Cyprian's Way

Compiled by

Laura Harris Stanger

Copyright © Laura Harris Stanger, 2013

All rights reserved. No parts of this book may be reproduced, stored in a retrieval system, or transmitted, in any form or by any means, electronic, mechanical, recording, or otherwise without the prior written permission of the author, except for purposes of a review, in which passages may be quoted in print, or broadcast on television or radio.

Cyprian's Way

ISBN 978-1-300-87241-2

Published by Laura Harris Stanger

Cover and layout by Mary Montague, m3m@rogers.com

> The picture on the front cover was captured by John Stanger in Southern Alberta. It serves to remind us that horses first appeared on the prairies in the mid-1700s, and that they have been important to Blackfoot families ever since.
>
> On the back cover is the original St. Cyprian's Anglican Church on the Peigan Reserve at Brocket Alberta. It is typical of those that first appeared on the prairies in the mid-1800s. In this picture, the Reverend C. Stanger is at the door.

Contents

FOREWORD

Cyprian: a Frontier Missionary 1

CHAPTER ONE

Blackfoot Country 7

CHAPTER TWO

Education of Alberta's Aborigines Prior to 1926 11

CHAPTER THREE

Thirty Years Later – 1956 19

NEWSLETTERS

St. Cyprian's Residential School 25

CHAPTER FOUR

School Term: 1956 - 1957 27

CHAPTER FIVE

School Term: 1957 - 1958 63

CHAPTER SIX

School Term: 1958 - 1959 103

CHAPTER SEVEN

Scrapbook 167

AFTERWORD 215

ACKNOWLEDGEMENTS

Thinking about my time at *St. Cyprian's Indian Residential School* I've come to realize why that junction on my long and winding life's trail was rather special. Indeed, it was a unique experience for me. *St. Cyprian's* was my home *and* my workplace - all under the same roof as sixty delightful First Nations pupils and a dozen precious staff members. I'm grateful to all those people for pleasant memories.

That 1950s experience was also special because it was shared by my family, and today I truly appreciate how Judith and John - who were children then - have shared my vision in the creation of *Cyprian's Way*. Their interest, their ideas, their input has kept their 89-year-old mom meandering in more or less the right direction. How blessed I am!

Preparing for the birth of *Cyprian's Way*, I turned - as I always do - to Mary. As my indispensable formatting artist, she established the final design of each page, and created the required cover for the book. Then she sent it off into cyberspace for printing. Without Mary's expertise there would be no *Cyprian's Way*. The standard *thank you* to such a talented person always seems so terribly inadequate, because my gratitude never wavers. Mary has shared my writing ventures for more than ten years, and has always done so cheerfully, carefully, and enthusiastically. Collaborations have been a joy, and I treasure her ongoing friendship.

Finally, to my readers. I want you to know that I've appreciated your interest, your kind words, your encouragement, and your support over the past two decades. Through my retirement writing and publishing ventures I have found new friends, and have re-establish contact with those of yesteryear. What could be more delightful!

DEDICATION

*"Cyprian's Way" is dedicated to the 1956-59
staff and pupils of
St. Cyprian's Indian Residential School*

*To each staff member whose sincere mission was
to inspire the Christian way of life, to teach academic
and practical life skills, and in every way possible serve
as a caring parent to the children in residence.*

*To each pupil who treasured
his or her inborn talents and basic education; who went
on to build upon that foundation, and in every way
possible made his or her home and community a better
place in which to live.*

Cyprian's Way is their story.

FOREWORD

Cyprian Pinkham

CYPRIAN: A FRONTIER MISSIONARY

Who is *Cyprian?* Indeed, what is a *frontier missionary?* To answer those questions, let us journey back in time and meet *William Cyprian Pinkham*, a frontier missionary whose name appears often in the book you are holding in your hands.

William Cyprian Pinkham was born in 1844 in St. John's Newfoundland. As a young man he went to England and studied theology at Cambridge University. As a newly-ordained deacon, he was selected by the *Society for the Propagation of the Gospel* to be a frontier missionary in the wilds of western Canada. As summarized below, he spent an extraordinary lifetime - always involved with both religious and academic education.

At age twenty-four, the Reverend Pinkham had reached North America and was making his way westward from Ontario to Manitoba, by way of Minnesota and North Dakota. When he arrived at Fort Abercrombie - a military outpost and transportation hub of the Red River Trail - he found that the traffic through there included wagon trains, stagecoaches, steamboats, and military supply wagons. There, at that junction, he met up with an official of the Hudson Bay Company who was traveling on to Winnipeg with his family, and they invited the young deacon to share their wagon and travel with them across the plains.

Cyprian describes that trek, and his life as a frontier missionary:

> *The journey from Fort Abercrombie to Winnipeg took two weeks, and the mosquitoes nearly ate us alive. Several horses, their long tails sweeping the ground, ran loose, and kept up with the wagon. There were streams to cross, but no bridges. That's when one of the extra horses would be caught and hitched by a knot in its tail in front of the horses that were in harness. Then with a sharp crack of a whip, we would get across the river and up the opposite bank. This worried me greatly until I learned that any horse used to that way of hauling pulls steadily and well, and there is no danger of its tail being pulled out!*

We travelled by easy stages. We slept in tents at night, and cooked our meals in the open as we needed them. On that journey we scarcely saw a human being except the members of our party. We came across what had once been a sparse settlement, but I was told it had been rendered extinct during the Sioux Massacre about five years earlier.

The Reverend Cyprian Pinkham remained the incumbent of St. James Anglican church in Winnipeg from 1868 to 1882, and then after being acting rector of All Saints for a year, he was appointed Archdeacon of Manitoba, and Canon of St. John's Cathedral.

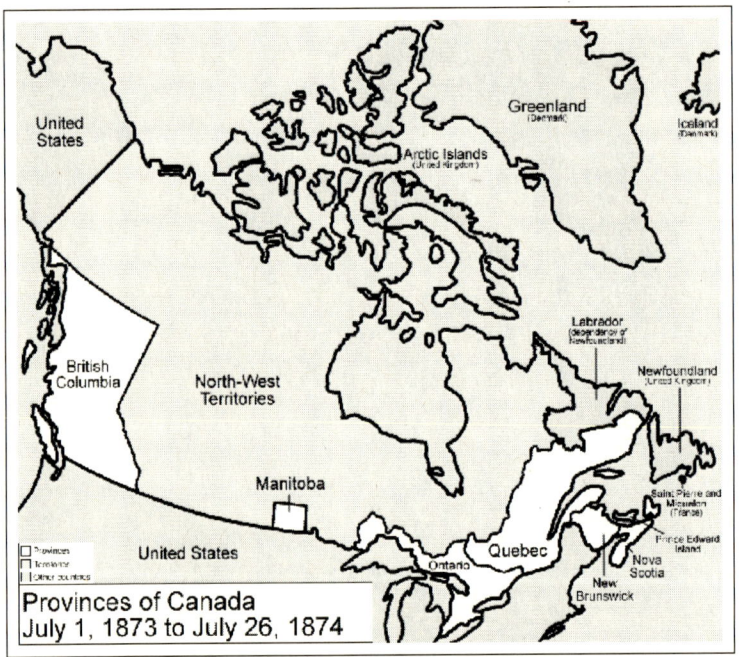

During my nineteen years in Winnipeg, the intersection of Portage Avenue and Main Street often became a quagmire of mud sufficient to swallow a man. The total population of 150 was scattered over a wide area in small dwellings of log and frame, completely surrounded by rich black loam.

In Winnipeg, Cyprian took on educational duties on top of his ministerial ones. He taught night school for boys three nights a week, and three nights a week for girls.

The zealous young Cyprian Pinkham wasted no time in getting himself a wife to share his missionary life. His future bride, Miss Jean Drever, was born in 1849 in the Red River Settlement of North Dakota. Jean's father was a Scottish Presbyterian carpenter from the Orkneys. Her mother was from Aberdeen but, as a young woman, had arrived in the Red River Settlement serving as a maid to the wife of a Hudson Bay Company official.

The third time Jean and Cyprian met, they became engaged. His annual missionary stipend was $720.00 but, as Jean said in her memoirs:

> *. . . he was young, energetic, impetuous, and didn't believe in losing any time. Thus, after a courtship of only two months, we were married on December 29, 1868, a bitterly cold day. I wore a soft white dress, a cloak and a small white bonnet. After a wedding breakfast, we drove sixteen miles in a cutter to our honeymoon destination.*

However, before that important day had arrived, Cyprian tells us he encountered a problem:

> *I had set about to find a suitable ring for my bride-to-be, but no such thing could be found anywhere. Finally, someone told me that there was a handy tinsmith in town who could make one for me out of a five-dollar gold piece. So I sent on to the tinsmith the money and the size of the bride's finger. The ring was made, and at our ceremony I slid it on her finger, a perfect fit. And there it remained always as good as new.*

When it became available, the couple moved into the St. James rectory, a home the nineteen-year-old Mrs. Pinkham described as *an adorable little bungalow* where they lived simply with handmade furnishings. She also tells in her memoirs how she felt about her new role:

> *I knew very little about being a clergyman's wife, but I put up a brave front, and taught Sunday school twice each Sunday. I had mothers' meetings, and a sewing class for girls. During the summer we had an annual gathering on our lawn, and for this I did all the cooking. We did a tremendous amount of visiting. With no nurses and few doctors, we had to do a lot of nursing; we often sat up night after night with a patient. On one occasion, sitting with a dear little boy who was very ill, it kept both of us busy keeping the bedbugs off him. They were all over the place; they were dropping from the ceiling.*

Cyprian's father-in-law, now a Winnipeg shop keeper, traded with the Indians and was very interested in their welfare. He delighted in telling this story:

> *One day there came to me a man saying he was very hungry and asking for food. The meal was provided, and he left. Many years later an Indian came to my door bearing a beautifully-dressed deer skin, and presented it to me. I did not understand why. The man said, "don't you remember that you gave food to a hungry Indian fifteen years ago? Well I am that Indian, and this skin is for you."*

Mrs. Pinkham, in her memoirs, describes a frontier shop, such as the one her father had:

> *At one end of the shop you could buy pemmican, dried meat, groceries, and at the other end some of the finest silks and wonderful bonnets. But there were never any wrappings; if you bought a pound of loose tea, you were asked what you wanted it put in. Often you had to buy a handkerchief for the purpose, and when the tea was dumped on it, it would be tied with a knot. If you also wanted a pound of sugar, it was put on top of that and another knot tied. If Indians were shopping, they would*

> *spread out their blankets on the counter and the groceries were tied up in them.*

Another peek into the life of a missionary in those days in taken from Rev. Pinkham's journal:

> *Riding or driving over the plains in Manitoba in all sorts of weather, in all seasons, and at all hours, I often arrived home early in the morning after hours of weary travel because the horse could not go at any pace but slow. Reaching home too tired to eat or go to bed all I could possibly do was stable the horse, and drop into a chair by the stove. Getting lost was a frequent occurrence even when I moved about in the most populated area of Winnipeg. Having most-inadequate winter clothing for temperatures that dropped to more than forty degrees below zero, I knew what it was like to be so cold I couldn't speak. Finally able to acquire a buffalo coat in 1876, I was never again frost-bitten in Manitoba.*

By now, the Reverend Pinkham was serving as Superintendent of Education for Protestant Schools of Manitoba, and as Chairman of the Board for the Northwest Territories. In addition, he traveled to study more progressive systems. He worked to establish teacher training courses, and a system of secondary education that could be linked to the University of Manitoba where he was an active member of council.

The Reverend and Mrs. Pinkham had 3 sons and 3 daughters, and their only help was one half-breed woman. Yet somehow that busy mother found time and stamina to be involved in the Women's Auxiliary, to have a class for girls at St. John's Ladies College, and to be president of the Women's Hospital Aid Society. The Pinkhams had many trying times, including the Riel Rebellion in 1870 when a number of their friends were taken prisoners. At times like that, it seems likely that Mrs. Pinkham would have, once again, relived the horrors she had experienced as a girl in North Dakota during the Sioux Massacre of 1862.

In 1887, Cyprian Pinkham was consecrated as The Second Bishop of Saskatchewan, and in 1888 as First Bishop of Calgary as well. The family moved to Calgary, Alberta - where, again, Cyprian was frost-bitten! In that city's juvenile years, Mrs. Pinkham worked to establish a hospital, and together the couple made many friends, including Prime Minister and Mrs. R.B. Bennett.

All of the above is a mere synopsis of the man who graduated from Cambridge University; who was known as *Chief Holy Rest* by the aborigines; who was missionary to Blackfoot natives, Hudson Bay Company personnel, and a variety of other pioneers in western Canada; who made arduous journeys to Eastern Canada and to Great Britain to seek knowledge and raise money to enhance religious and educational work in the west. Indeed, during his sixty year ministry, Cyprian Pinkham blazed a trail and set a standard for all who dared to follow.

Peigan Reserve, Brocket, Alberta

CHAPTER ONE

BLACKFOOT COUNTRY

East of the Rocky Mountains has long been known as Blackfoot country. Indeed, history tells us it was Blackfoot country back in 10,000 BC when aborigines of North America were hunting *mammoth,* an elephant-like beast that became extinct some 4,000 years later.

The name *Blackfoot* comes from the native word *Siksika* meaning, *I am Blackfoot.* In the mid-1700s exclusive Blackfoot country covered 80,000 square miles, and at that time the aborigines lived nomadic lives following the great buffalo herds that supplied their food, shelter, and entertainment. Buffalo meat gave them strength and they used buffalo hides to make tepees and clothing to protect them from the harsh climate. The Blackfoot used dogs to tote their supplies from place to place, and their most essential and basic tools were knives.

The North Peigan (Piikani) discussed in this book is a First Nation group that shares membership in the Blackfoot Confederacy along with The Blood (Kainai), the Blackfoot (Siksika), and the South Peigan[1] of Montana.

For 200 years, the natives carried on an active fur-trading business with the Hudson Bay Company (HBC) throughout a vast area then known as *Rupert's Land* - millions of square kilometers that would one day become part of Manitoba, Alberta, Saskatchewan, Ontario and Quebec.

However, that fur-trading business was disrupted when the Hudson Bay Company's official control of Rupert's Land ended, and that entire area became part of the new Dominion of Canada. This sudden change of authority over the natives' hunting grounds not only disrupted their fur-trade business, but it created unrest throughout the area. Indeed, it caused the Dominion of Canada's first crisis, the Red River Rebellion of 1869 - 1870.

To study the problem in the west, Sir John A. Macdonald sent a fact-finding team to Rupert's Land, and that study resulted in the formation of

---

1 *The **South Peigans** are frequently referred to as **South Piegans**.*

the North West Mounted Police (NWMP). Five hundred and fifty mounted riflemen were trained, and the new force began marching west with its carts, wagons, field guns, and beef on the hoof. The mandate of the NWMP was to keep order and protect surveyors and railway builders who were working their way towards the Pacific. At Fort Macleod - named in honour of Colonel Macleod - they set up a permanent NWMP post, and from that moment on they were also in control of migration.

> Jerry Potts was born Kyyokosi in 1840. He was the son of Namopisi, a Montana aboriginal woman and Andrew R. Potts, a Scottish fur-trader. Jerry learned to read and write, and he knew how to live with both native and white people. He could speak English, Blackfoot, and Crow. When he chose to do so, he could also communicate in Cree, Sioux and Algonkian.

> Dressed like a white man or wearing buckskin, Jerry wore a fedora on his head. As a warrior, he toted a couple .44 pistols, a rifle, a long-bladed skinning knife, and always another small gun hidden in his clothing. Potts was a mountain man, a cowboy, and a horse-trader who roamed the country and knew it well. He was welcomed into the Blackfoot Nation as a Peigan War Chief.

Jerry Potts

> In 1871, when the North West Mounted Police became totally lost on their initial trek from Ontario to the western frontier, it was the 31-year-old Peigan War Chief Jerry Potts who rescued them.

> Potts was hired by the NWMP as a guide, interpreter, and scout. He was given a 22-year contract at $90.00 a month

- three times the regular police salary at the time. However, it seems he was worth it. His integrity and loyalty never faltered. He guided Colonel Macleod and the NWMP to Fort Whoop-Up, and there the force shut down the illegal practice of trading whiskey for furs - a practice that was destroying a great many aboriginal fur-traders.

At age 56, Jerry Potts died in Macleod, Alberta, and was given full honors for his twenty-two years of service as a special constable of the Mounties.

With the disruption of the fur-trade business, the beginning of colonization, and depleted buffalo herds, the natives were destined to die unless their livelihood could be obtained in a different way. That different way of life came with the signing of *Treaty Seven* on September 22, 1877.

Treaty Seven was an agreement between the natives and the government of Canada, and it was that agreement which effectively gathered Alberta's natives on to reserves where they could use their land for farming or ranching.

The Peigan Indian Reserve No. 147 (Piikani Nation) situated along the Old Man River near Pincher Creek and west of Lethbridge in southwestern Alberta, covered approximately 180 square miles with 7000 acres for farming and ranching. And there, the Piikani Nation grew wheat and hay, and raised cattle and horses.

CHAPTER TWO

EDUCATION OF ALBERTA'S ABORIGINES PRIOR TO 1926

When Alberta's aborigines lived nomadic lives their children did not go to a school. Their classroom was the natural environment. Their teachers were their elders. Their course of studies included all the practical skills of being a nomad; of living a life controlled by the laws of nature, and by the laws of their ancestors and their Creator. The desired result of practicing those skills and embracing those values was survival - survive to live nomadic lives following the massive herds of buffalo that ruled western grasslands before colonization.

However, as immigrants began to settle in Canada and move west, missionaries and churches began to try to provide religious and academic training to the natives. By 1840 a variety of religious organizations were doing what they could to educate aboriginal children.

Prior to Confederation in 1867, the Anglican missions in remote British North America had three primary objectives: to evangelize local native populations, to administer to the sick, and to provide basic schooling for the young. Many young Indians were baptized, confirmed by the Church, and educated in European and Church traditions.

Under the terms of the Constitution Act, the subsequent Indian Act of 1876, and various other numbered treaties with first nation groups in the west, the new Canadian government was obliged to provide schooling for aboriginal children. Soon other aggressive policies prompted the regulation of educational methods and ultimate assimilation of the natives.

Following the signing of Treaty Seven in 1877, a greater urgency developed for the education of western native children, and Anglican missionary activity began among the three Canadian Blackfoot nations, as well as the Sarcee (Tsuu Tina). Funding came from the Church Missionary Society (CMS) and later the Missionary Society of the Church of England in Canada (MSCC).

St. Peter's Mission:

The Reverend George McKay, an Anglican missionary funded by the Church Missionary Society (CMS), arrived in Fort Macleod in 1878, and soon established a little day school at Brocket on the new Peigan Reserve where native Piikani families were beginning to settle. However, it wasn't long until St. Peter's Mission had to admit and care for children unable to live at home.

In 1884 the *Indian Act* was amended to make school mandatory for all native children under the age of sixteen. As a result, the government of Canada provided funding for the running of the schools and led an expansion in the number of **church-run Indian residential schools** from 11 schools in 1880 to 45 by 1896. At its peak involvement in the late 1920s, the Anglican Church concurrently operated 24 schools situated mostly in northern regions of central and western Canada. Students in the Anglican schools were supported materially and financially by the

Missionary Society of the Church of England in Canada (MSCC), the Women's Auxiliary (WA) and by non-native parishes that were asked to sponsor a child. Canada's other major Christian churches had similar roles in educating aboriginal peoples.

When the Anglican Diocese of Calgary was created in 1888, it was made responsible for the pastoral and educational work of natives, and the Calgary Indian Mission agency was put in charge of coordinating this work. Two years later, St. Peter's Mission was replaced by The Peigan Mission Home.

The Peigan Mission Home:

Peigan Mission Home

This 1890 boarding school had room for a dozen boarders, but three years later had to be expanded to accommodate 36 residential pupils. During this time, Roman Catholic missionaries were also actively involved throughout the Blackfoot Confederacy, and on the Peigan Reserve in the mid-1890s the Grey Nuns began teaching at the Sacred Heart Residential School. Because the Peigan Mission Home was viewed as substandard and quite obviously unable to accommodate the number of Protestant boarders needing care, the Diocese of Calgary and Indian Affairs agreed to construct a substantial new residential school.

The Victoria Jubilee Home for Indian Children:

Victoria Jubilee Home

The area's first residential school - with the Reverend H.D. Bourne as principal - was officially opened in 1897 by the Governor General of Canada, the Duke of Aberdeen. It was named in honour of Queen Victoria whose Diamond Jubilee was being celebrated that year. Located in the Old Man River valley near Pincher Creek, the school had space for 30 residential pupils. However, in 1909 dormitory space had to be expanded.

In 1911 Ottawa and the Diocese of Calgary agreed to certain standards for residential school admissions, and to specific requirements for school buildings. The government would pay an annual per capita grant of $100 for each student. However, overcrowding continued, and relations between school administrators and government agents became strained because contracts were not being adhered to by school staff.

In addition to overcrowding at the Victoria Jubilee Home, the 20-year-old building was suffering extensive water damage due to frequent spring flooding of the Old Man River. In 1917, with the building in a state of disrepair and due for closure, the Church and local Peigan elders petitioned the federal government to build a new residential school on higher ground that would be large enough to accommodate 50 pupils.

In 1920, the Missionary Society of the Church of England in Canada (MSCC) took over the work conducted by the Calgary Indian Missions, and that included the Victoria Jubilee Home and other Anglican boarding schools. The MSCC's Indian and Eskimo School Commission provided all administrative support and funding, and by 1923 most all Anglican Indian residential schools in Canada were under MSCC control.

Some of the children who gained basic academic education at *The Victoria Jubilee Home for Indian Children* were:

Frank Four Horns	Joseph Medicine Calf	Joe Small Legs
Jim Morning Bull	Albert Runaway Buffalo	Bob Crow Eagle
Samson Knowlton	Dick Runaway Buffalo	George Baptiste
Joey Cold Weather	Jack Crow	Willie Knowlton
Sam Little Bear	Harold Sharp Adze	Tom Yellow Horn
Edward White Mustache		Amy Dog Killer
Sarah Mouse	Susie Warrior	Nora One Crow
Ethel Wolf Robe	Emma Wolf Tail	

St. Cyprian's Indian Residential School:

The new larger residential school that had been requested by Peigan elders opened in 1926. It had space for fifty pupils, and it was on higher ground just four km southeast of Brocket on the Peigan Reserve. St. Cyprian's Indian Residential School was named in honour of the first Bishop of Calgary, the Rt. Rev. William Cyprian Pinkham who had just retired after a sixty-year ministry on the prairies where he had always been deeply involved in both religious and academic education.

All of St. Cyprian's residential pupils came from homes on the Peigan Reserve and, since the school had a working farm, the boys received some training in agriculture, gardening, and raising cattle. The girls acquired basic skills in cooking, baking, laundry and sewing. All learned about caring for their surroundings.

The approved provincial public school curriculum was taught by teachers hired by the government. The direct family care of the children in residence was provided by missionary workers sponsored by the Church Missionary Society. Teachers and all other staff members lived within the school. All worked together to create a caring home, school, church, and community for the children in their care, as well as providing various activities for pre-schoolers and adults on the reserve.

Pupils who transferred from *The Victoria Jubilee School for Indian Children* to the new *St. Cyprian's Indian Residential School* were:

Mike One Owl	Allan Prairie Chicken	Fred Iron Shirt
Mick Crazy Boy	Joe Crow Shoe	George Big Weasel
James Chickie	Tom Big Smoke	Edward Meat Face
Tommy Bull Pen	Eldred Small Legs	Hartwell North Peigan
Ned Muggins	*Richard Crow Shoe	William Red Young Man
Pete Warrior	Henry Warrior	
Elizabeth Big Bull	Maggie Knowlton	Annie Mouse
Nellie Yellow Horn	Rosie Spear	Lucy Warrior
Josephine Warrior	Mona Crazy Boy	Mary North Peigan
Agnes North Peigan	Maggie Big Swan	Lily Shinning Double
Molly Little Plume	Philomene Woodman	

* "On that June day," said Richard, "it was raining so hard that the creek was flooded. All the girls were transported in a wagon pulled by four horses. The little boys were driven the distance by the principal. But the big boys had to walk the whole six miles."

The newly constructed 1926 St.Cyprian's school and a handsome 20th century vehicle.

The back of the school.

CHAPTER THREE

THIRTY YEARS LATER – 1956

The Stanger Family Arrive at St. Cyprian's

Charles, Laura, Judith and John Stanger with Yukon vehicle in front of St. Cyprian's in southern Alberta.

Laura's Personal View

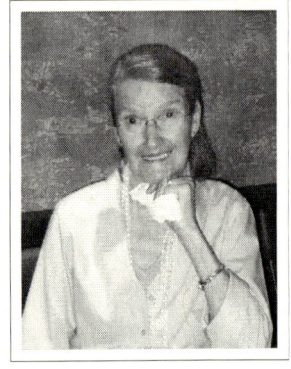

The Canadian part of North America's Rocky Mountain range dominates the landscape of Alberta, British Columbia, and the Yukon; and in one way or another the mountains affect the lives of all who live and work and play in those areas.

It is said that the Rockies make Alberta one of the most beautiful places on earth. However, no matter who claims what, the Rockies are impressive. They are beguiling. When viewed from a distance, they are picturesque. When traveling through them by highway or railway, they are both menacing and awesome. Mountain scenery is always changing; always projecting a different view that causes a different impression.

Early in 1946 my personal status had changed: from single to married, and from airwoman to civilian. Forevermore I would be a veteran of World War Two. Officially and honorably discharged from the RCAF in Ottawa, I went by train - the local Push, Pull and Jerk - to Shawville, Quebec. There I visited my parents and siblings, gathered up some warm civilian clothing, and booked my journey to Whitehorse, Yukon, with the help of the local stationmaster - a man who was thrilled to do so, and determined to get it right. You see, he had never before arranged transportation from Shawville to the Yukon.

I crossed Canada by train to Edmonton, Alberta, and from there my flight to Whitehorse was by Canadian Pacific Airlines. Assigned a window seat, I was delighted; my first look at the Rocky Mountains would be amazing. Yes, that's what I thought. But from thousands of feet above terra firma, all I could see from my tiny window was snow - an endless mass of snow that covered whatever was hibernating beneath such a great rumpled blanket.

I arrived in Whitehorse in the dark, and soon learned that Yukon winters remain dark day and night, month after month. Nevertheless, summer finally did arrive, and then - as if by magic - my world was enclosed by beautiful, majestic mountain peaks, and surrounded by mountain valleys carpeted in wildflowers. Being a farm girl from the gently-rolling slopes of the Ottawa Valley, I was amazed. I was enchanted.

A few years later when my home was near the village of Carcross, also in the Yukon, my kitchen window faced a mountain that looked like a large open book. We called it *Book Mountain*. There, far away from family and friends, that mountain was like a good neighbour. It stabilized my world. It provided daily diversion and inspiration. In some mystical way *Book Mountain* cheered and comforted me. And you know, that magnificent rock formation gave me courage to do things I'd never done before - such as making supper for my family using fresh bear meat.

(More about life in the Yukon is contained in my book "Echo" published in 2011 and in "Laughing Water" published in 2012)

By 1956, however, a move south seemed a wise and necessary step in the social development of our two young children. We were proud of our accomplishments in the north, and of the beautiful new residential school that was built while we were there. So, being comfortably employed under the umbrella of *the Indian School Administration* (I.S.A.), we were pleased when that agency's Canon Cook arranged for our move to another residential school in southern Alberta.

I had to say goodbye to *Book Mountain*. But as we drove from the Yukon to our new assignment we did not leave the Rockies behind. Oh no, they were with us every inch of the way from Mile 918 at Whitehorse to the southernmost end of the Alaska Highway. However, on that drive, the mountains gave me not one moment of comfort, not one iota of pleasure. To be honest I was terrified the whole way.

To begin with, we were trapped inside a vehicle that kept bouncing through potholes and slithering around on loose gravel. Mile after dusty mile of that winding trail presented a wall of jagged rock on one side, and a sharp drop off to the depths below on the other side. Guardrails? Not one. I had visions of sudden death; one false move or one misjudged curve would either impale us on those lethal rocks, or plunge us straight down into a bottomless wilderness valley. The early Alaska Highway was not for the feint of heart.

Nevertheless, we finally arrived at our destination near the Canada-United States border. Here, again stood the same 150-million-year-old Rocky Mountain range looking like a picturesque mural hanging on the western sky. Although the peaks were many miles away, the foothills presented a delightful agricultural scene that rolled gently upward towards the mountains.

It was August 16, 1956, when we - Charles, Laura, Judith and John Stanger - arrived at St. Cyprian's Indian Residential School on the Peigan Indian Reserve. And even though that happened fifty-seven years ago, I can still hop on to my magic carpet and be right back there again.

• • •

It is a hot summer's day, and the four of us are sticking to the seats of our light blue vehicle that is now dusty inside and out. Our traveling clothes are rumpled and moist, and I know we aren't going to generate a great first impression this day.

Even though our vehicle still has the words *Carcross Indian School* printed on both sides, that particular school - our beautiful *Chooutla* - is now more than a thousand miles away in the mountains of the Yukon. And now, here I sit looking at a plain three-story building. Here I sit thinking, *This place can't be a school; it is just a big old shoe box....* Then, as an experienced homemaker, I wonder: W*here are we going to live? Do I have to try and make a cosy nest for my family somewhere in that building? ... Yes, I know there was once an old woman who lived in a shoe - every child knows that one - but is our home going to be in a corner of that big old shoe box?*

Suddenly, I feel sure that people are peering through the windows of the shoe box. *Oh, oh! I bet they're wondering what that strange vehicle is doing in their yard; wondering why those people are just sitting there like four sticks of wood.* Obviously, they can't know that we're clinging to the only familiar space we've had during this transition; they can't know that we aren't even sure we're at our correct destination.

Nevertheless, there is only one thing to do. So we push open the two big doors, place our feet on the prairies, grasp the hands of our children, and climb the big wide steps leading up to the main door.

Inside, we're assured we are at *St. Cyprian's Indian Residential School.* We introduce ourselves. We are welcomed. We're shown the rooms on the main floor that are for our private use. *Private?* Our bedrooms are on one side of the school's main hallway; our kitchen, dining room, living room, and bathroom are on the opposite side. *Oh my! Who will dare to dart across that thoroughfare in pajamas?* Then wandering through our potential dining room, I look out a window, and right there behind the school I see a barn, sheds, a field, cattle, a garden.... *Glory be! I'm back on a farm, but where are the trees?*

• • •

In time our nest was made. All that had been strange in the beginning became comfortable. With a large family of school children, and with abundant and diverse duties our days became extremely full. Life was interesting. Work was rewarding. Our children went to their classes along with the residential children. John's classroom was on the main floor with the grade two pupils, and Judith's grade four was on the second floor.

There in that land of the chinook, the wind blew. It forced its way around the windows and through every crack and crevice in the building. One day while talking on the phone to my mom who lived halfway across Canada, she said, "There's an awfully loud whistling sound on this line today."

"Oh, really?" I replied, as casually as possible. "Maybe it's just because the wind is blowing." I wasn't about to tell her that our building was swaying in the wind. She would have worried about us. If she could have looked through the dining room window and seen how giant restraining cables were struggling against the force of the wind, she would have been frantic.

And that makes me recall: Sharing a meal with the school staff the day we arrived, one of the men - Mr. Irwin, I think it was - said, "I see you all have lots of hair on the top of your heads, but mark my words, it won't be there for long." We newcomers, I feel sure, hadn't a clue what that was all about, and we just sat there staring at him. "Well, just look at this," he said patting the top of his head. "Hair used to cover this patch of skin ... yes, indeed, 'twas a fine head of hair I had.... But here the wind blows ... the building sways ... my bed rocks ... my head rubs against the top of the bed, and it's goodbye hair."

During those early days at St. Cyprian's, I found that the Alberta mountains - as seen in the distance from my dining room window - kept my thoughts going back to *Book Mountain* that stood just outside my kitchen window in the Yukon. I would think of how the mountains in the Yukon had held us close; how they had dominated our daily lives and isolated us from the *outside world. In southern Alberta, it seemed obvious that the Rockies were not going to isolate us from anything. Life would be different.

Yes, indeed, those mountains gracing the western horizon told me we would now have easy access by highway from the Peigan Reserve to other communities in Canada and the United States. When we were free to do so, we might visit interesting and historic places such as Fort Macleod, 20 miles east; Pincher Creek, 16 miles west; Lethbridge, 38 miles east. We could go to a theater and see a movie, or go bicycling across the prairies. We could pack a picnic lunch and drive to the mountains, perhaps west to Crowsnest Pass, or south to Waterton Lakes National Park.

However, as a newcomer, I had no idea how much our world would open up, and I could not foresee exactly how that openness would, so

very gently, introduce our children to *their outside[2] world*. But what I did know, without a doubt, was that the Rocky Mountains would never cease to enchant me.

---

2 *The word outside is used by northerners when referring to all more-southern and more-settled parts of North America.*

NEWSLETTERS
St. Cyprian's Residential School

CHAPTER FOUR

SCHOOL TERM: 1956 - 1957

TO FAMILIES AND FRIENDS OF ST. CYPRIAN'S
as taken from our first St. Cyprian's Newsletter, September, 1956

We, the Stanger family, arrived here at St. Cyprian's about one month ago to take over from the Reverend Miller and family, and to get ready for the new 1956-57 school term. We've settled into our apartment on the main floor of the school, and we've become acquainted with ten staff members: the matron, two teachers, two supervisors, two assistants, the cook, the farmer, and the maintenance man. Next came the pupils: 33 girls and 22 boys - our new family complete! This is a new beginning for everyone here, and it is another opportunity for each of us to enjoy personal growth and new endeavours.

One new endeavour is to produce a school newsletter. Of course we've decided to call it St. Cyprian's Newsletter because its main purpose is to keep families and friends of St. Cyprian's school and of St. Cyprian's church up-to-date with our activities. Students and staff members are the reporters.

In this first newsletter, we newcomers want to extend our greetings to the parents of our pupils, to all who attend St. Cyprian's church, and to all families living on the Peigan Reserve. We look forward to meeting each of you as time goes by.

In the meantime, however, perhaps you would like to know that the Stanger family includes your principal and rector Charles Stanger, his wife Laura, daughter Judith, and son John. We were transferred here from Carcross, Yukon, where we enjoyed five years at Chooutla Indian Residential School in a magnificent wilderness mountain setting.

On our way here, we had a stopover in Edmonton, and then we went sightseeing in Calgary, Radium Hot Springs, Lake Louise,

Banff, Cranbrook, Kicking Horse Pass - and everything in between. Along the roads in the mountains we counted twenty-three black bears, and some of them were kind enough to came close to our car so we could take their pictures.

It seems that the school year has just begun, but a holiday is coming up soon. We ask all the parents of our pupils to please take note:

Thanksgiving Holiday! There will be no classes between October 4 and October 9. The Thanksgiving Day holiday is Monday, October 8, but as our teachers are attending a convention on Oct. 4 and 5, **children may go home after class October 3, and return during the afternoon of October 8.**

HAPPY THANKSGIVING TO ALL!

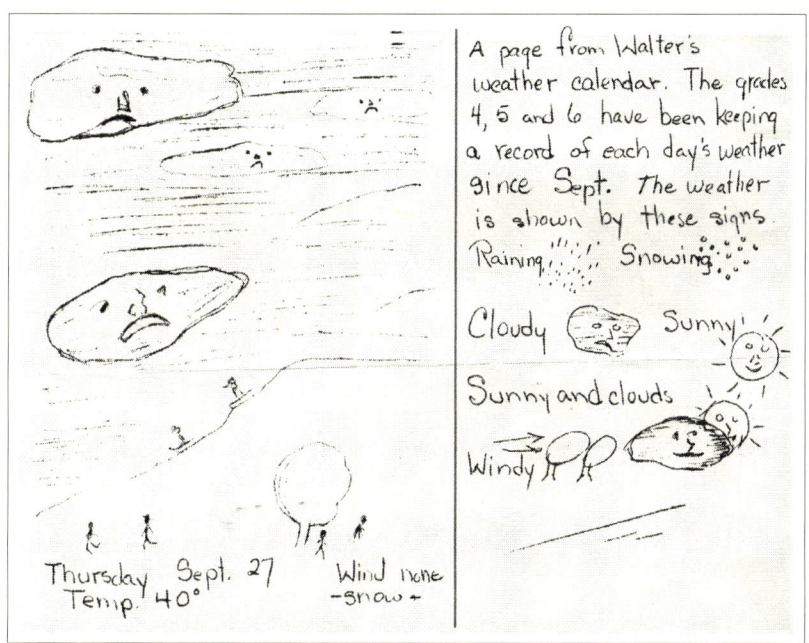

Weather map by Walter Crow Shoe

OUR SCHOOL by George Crow Shoe, grade 8
as taken from St. Cyprian's Newsletter, September, 1956

Our school is four miles south of Brocket, and it is pretty big. There is a big farm connected with the school. Harvesting has started, and Mr. Irwin has said that there is a good crop this year.

Last year we had a 4-H calf club here, and each of the nine senior boys had a calf. We have sports here too. We play softball, football, etc. and hockey in winter.

THIS AND THAT, by Elizabeth Crow Flagg, grade 8
as taken from St. Cyprian's Newsletter, September, 1956

The Reverend H.B. Miller and his family were transferred to Old Sun School at Gleichen at the end of July. He was only principal here at St. Cyprian's for the past year. The Reverend C. T. Stanger is now principal here.

Miss Dawn Dickenson left the school. She was one of the staff last year, but she will be going to work in British Columbia. Miss E. Bayne has come to take her place. She worked in the Indian School at Edmonton last year.

Sharon Crow Shoe and Elizabeth Crow Flagg were at camp with a C.G.I.T. group at Waterton Lake for one week this summer.

Cadet Wayne Knowlton went to Army Cadet camp at Vernon, B.C. for two weeks this summer.

A new little boy and girl have started school this fall. They are Johnny Iron Shirt and Linda Yellow Horn. Melinda Red Young Man has started too.

Mrs. Ellis just came back from the hospital. She was there for three weeks, but now she is alright and back at work as girls' supervisor.

Lena Warrior, Delbert and Wallace Yellow Face, Veronica and Louis Crow Eagle are no longer at St. Cyprian's. They are attending day school in Brocket. We hope they will enjoy it there.

Lewis Strikes With A Gun graduated from here last June and has gone to live at St. Paul's School, Cardston. We hope he has a successful year in grade nine, and will like it very much.

PEIGAN CADET CORPS by Roderick North Peigan, grade 8
as taken from St. Cyprian's Newsletter, September, 1956

We started going to cadets last January. Five of us went then, but there are only three of us going this school year. Mr. Stanger takes Wayne Knowlton, George Crow Shoe, and myself on Thursday nights.

There are some boys there from Sacred Heart School and from day schools. A large group of boys from Pincher Creek also come. Our instructors are Sergeant Bowen and Sergeant Parkins.

MY TRIP TO SUMMER CAMP by Wayne Knowlton, grade 8
as taken from St. Cyprian's Newsletter, September, 1956

We started out on Wednesday afternoon, July 4, at 6 p.m. Gerald Smith and Frank Holloway were with me. We took the bus to Macleod and to Calgary. We slept at the armory in Calgary that night.

Early next day the cadets from Calgary and other places joined us and we took the train to Vernon, B.C. We traveled all day. That night we got to Salmon Arm, which is about forty miles from Vernon. The army buses were waiting for us there and we got to Vernon at midnight.

The next morning we got up at 6 a.m. Boy, was I tired. There were fifty-eight cadets, and they had to divide us into our huts and platoons. There were five Indian boys and twenty-seven white boys in my hut.

Every day after supper we were free to go to town or to the beach. We had supper at 5 p.m., and I always went swimming after. My friend Frank Holloway was sick and had to stay in bed the first week.

The night before we went home, there was a party. I went with Gerald Smith and we stayed until 11 p.m. Everybody had hotdogs, watermelon, and pop.

We got up at three o'clock the next morning, had breakfast at four, and then took the bus to Salmon Arm. We arrived back home on Saturday night, July 17.

OUR WEEK AT CAMP by Sharon Crow Shoe, grade 6

as taken from St. Cyprian's Newsletter, September, 1956

Elizabeth Crow Flagg and I spent a week this summer at Canyon Church Camp at Waterton Park. We enjoyed ourselves very much.

We took the bus from Brocket and arrived at Waterton on Monday afternoon, July 16. We lived in cabins while we were there. There were 15 girls in ours.

We took turns doing the chores. In the mornings, we washed dishes, swept floors, and peeled potatoes. In the afternoons, we went swimming or went for hikes. After supper, we had camp fires and all sat around and sang songs. We also roasted marshmallows.

We came home the next Monday after a very happy week.

Opening day of hunting season by a grade 4 boy.

THIS AND THAT by Evelyn Crazy Boy, grade 8
as taken from St. Cyprian's Newsletter, October, 1956

All the pupils enjoyed their Thanksgiving holiday very much. The teachers went to the convention in Lethbridge, while most of the other members of staff went away for a day or two.

Tuesday night, grades six, seven and eight went to a show in Fort Macleod. The show was very interesting, and it was called Helen of Troy.

Regular classes of handicrafts, Girls' Auxiliary, Junior Auxiliary, sewing, and Sunday school have all started.

The harvest is finished and the potatoes were picked last Tuesday. Roderick and George are going to help bring the cattle from the range. Johnny Weasel Bear and Norman Big Smoke have been helping Mr. Irwin with the hay bales to get finished before winter catches them.

We have had new linoleum put on the stairs and a few other repairs done inside and outside of the school.

Miss Sylvia Curtis, who once worked here, was a visitor here for a few days.

Mr. Andy Brown is on holidays. He is visiting in Calgary, Grande Prairie and DeBolt.

PICKING POTATOES by Mildred Woodman, grade 4
as taken from St. Cyprian's Newsletter, October, 1956

Last Tuesday morning we went out to pick potatoes. Everybody had a pail. Those who went were from grades two to eight.

Mr. Irwin was on the tractor digging them up, and everybody would run behind him and race for the potatoes. It was fun. We finished early and came back to the school. The children who didn't go were coming from class for recess. We all went back to class after recess.

SENIOR CLASSROOM NOTES by Agnes Strikes With A Gun, grade 6
as taken from St. Cyprian's Newsletter, October, 1956

Grades six, seven and eight have study groups every Tuesday night.

Miss Koski, our teacher, bought four tonettes. We are learning to play them.

We made kites last Wednesday. We tried to fly them, and had fun with them.

We have physical training Tuesdays and Thursdays. Miss Koski takes the boys and Miss Crow Shoe takes the girls.

Each week we have two policemen. They put a mark against us when we don't follow the good conduct rules. We get stars if we have no marks.

We listen to the radio broadcasts for some of our singing and drawing lessons.

OUR SCHOOL ROOM by Judith Stanger, grade 4
as taken from St. Cyprian's Newsletter, October, 1956

One day when the big boys and girls were out killing chickens, we made up a show. The boys sang Billy Boy and some other songs. The girls played nurse, and I was sick! I didn't like that. When the show ended, I was better. That was good.

Miss Koski read us a book about Ben Franklin, and then she read Black Beauty, and today she started Heide Grows Up.

BIG NEWS! by Patsy Yellow Horn, grade 3
as taken from St. Cyprian's Newsletter, October, 1956

We have a T.V. in Miss How's classroom! Sometimes we can look at it.

We have a big doll. Her name is Jenny. And we have two more dolls. One is Joyce. The other one's name is Snow White.

DID YOU KNOW?
excerpts from St. Cyprian's Newsletter of October, 1956

- During the past ten years the number of Indian children attending school has more than doubled, while the number attending High School has increased ten times. Many are studying to be teachers, nurses, stenographers and tradesmen.

- Mr. R.F. Davey, Superintendent of Indian Education for Indian Affairs employs nine stenographers, and five of them are Canadian Indians.

- Scientists guess that before the white man arrived in America, there were about 225,000 aborigines living in the part of North America that is Canada.

A SMILE from Miss How's 1956 junior classroom:

On Tuesday, one of the little girls in Miss How's classroom asked her teacher, "Who are the bannisters?"

Miss How explained, "The banisters are the railings on the stairs; those things you hold on to when you go up or down."

But that didn't satisfy the little girl. She grew impatient. "But who are the bannisters this week?"

Finally, it all became clear to Miss How. What her conscientious little pupil really wanted to know was who is going to stand by the stairs and watch that nobody runs.

Junior Classroom News: by Miss How, teacher

We have two new pupils. Harvey Plain Eagle and Louis Crow Eagle.

Oliver Crow Eagle went to the hospital yesterday to get the cast off his arm. Valerie Crow Shoe went to have her tonsils out.

Kenneth, Caroline, and Linda Yellow Horn have a new baby sister.

Sandra and Diane North Peigan have a new baby brother.

Louisa Crow Shoe and Sandra North Peigan are leading the class on our star chart. They each have eight stars.

WE FOLLOW CANADA'S FOOD RULES
as written in St. Cyprian's Newsletter, November, 1956

How does it happen?

How does it happen?

It's strange, but it's true

That what you have eaten

Is turned into you

Whether it's beef, or a lettuce leaf,

Raw tomatoes, baked potatoes,

Oranges, cherries, wild strawberries

Curly greens, straight string beans,

Butter, bread, an apple red,

Peppers, peas, milk or cheese,

You chew and swallow,

You swallow and chew,

And what you have eaten

Is turned into YOU!

We Try To Eat These Foods Every Day:

1) 3 different kinds of vegetables.

2) 2 kinds of fruit.

3) 3 glasses of milk or foods made with milk.

4) A helping of meat or fish, or a food made with dried peas, beans, peanuts, or an egg.

5) Cereal for breakfast. Bread, toast, rolls, or muffins with enriched margarine at every meal

6) *Vitamin D in cod liver oil or a vitamin pill.*

THE 4-H CALF CLUB

The 4-H Club has been around since the 1930s. It has always remained geared to helping young people to become productive citizens, by instructing them in useful skills related to agriculture, animal husbandry, community services, and personal development. Competing at a fall fair or other venue is a big event, and it is a proud moment for both the member and his or her parents when a coveted prize is won.

The Aim of the club today, as it has always been for eighty-odd years, remains fourfold: to improve **head**, **heart**, **hands** and **health**.

Here at the school, the club was initiated by the Reverend Harry B. Miller in 1955. The following is what he wrote in his message to parishioners of St. Cyprian's Anglican Church in Brocket in his newsletter dated November 21, 1955:

> We now have a 4-H Calf Club which takes in both St. Cyprian's and Sacred Heart schools. There are three boys from Sacred Heart and six boys from St. Cyprian's looking after calves. St. Cyprian's boys are Roderick North Peigan, George Crow Shoe, Dalbert Yellow Face, Joseph Crow Shoe, Wayne Knowlton, Lewis Strikes With A Gun. At present we just have three calves, but we hope to get three more so that each boy will have a calf. The boys are going to look after the calves until next summer and then we shall have a competition with the Sacred Heart school to see which boy raised the best calf. The winner will get a heifer as the prize to start a herd of his own. When the calves are sold the boys will be able to have the money that the calves make at the sale. So far the boys are doing very well as they have the calves halter broke and are able to lead them to water.

OUR BICYCLES by George Crow Shoe, grade 8
as taken from St. Cyprian's Newsletter, November, 1956

As most of you know, the senior boys from St. Cyprian's have bicycles. We bought them with the money we made from our 4-H calf club. The bicycles come in handy because we go home on them Fridays and come back on them on Sundays.

FAREWELL PARTY by Wayne Knowlton, grade 8
as taken from St. Cyprian's Newsletter, November, 1956

The Peigan W.A. held a party at the Community Hall on Wednesday night, November 28. There were about 130 people there. It was in honour of Mr. John Irwin who is leaving St. Cyprian's after being here for over eighteen years. We will miss him very much.

A gift was presented to him by Mr. Stanger on behalf of the staff of the school, the people of the reserve and Brocket. Elizabeth gave him a pair of socks, which she had knit, from the girls. I presented a wallet made by the boys, from all the boys.

The other guest of honour was Rev. Eric Scott of Pincher Creek. He is leaving there this month to go to Edmonton. Evelyn Crow Shoe presented a gift to him.

Mr. Irwin and Mr. Scott made speeches of thank you. We ended the party by singing, "For They Are Jolly Good Fellows" and "Auld Lang Syne."

THIS AND THAT
from St. Cyprian's Newsletter, November, 1956

Mr. Kester, who has replaced Mr. Waller as Indian School Inspector, visited us last Thursday.

In October, several people from this reserve were in a serious accident. Little Patrick Crow Shoe, age 5, lost his life in it. His brothers Walter and Robert are at school here and we extend our sympathy to them. Mr. Joe Buffalo was quite badly injured and is still in the Camsell Hospital. We are glad to hear that Mrs. Joe Buffalo, Mr. Joe Crow Shoe and Mr. Jim Plain Eagle have recovered from their injuries and are now at home.

Mr. Brown and Mr. Irwin have put up a new fence around the playgrounds. There is a new slide on the girl's playground.

Some new hockey equipment has arrived. The boys are anxiously waiting for cold weather and ice to make use of it.

One night Mr. Stanger showed us some slides of the Yukon. We enjoyed them very much.

Several people on the reserve have mumps. We're hoping we don't get them here at the school.

Ada Buffalo was in the hospital for a few days, but is back again.

OUR HALLOWE'EN PARTY by Evelyn Crazy Boy, grade 8
as taken from St. Cyprian's Newsletter, November, 1956

Our senior party was organized by Miss Higgins and Miss Crow Shoe, and was held in the boys' dayroom.

We played relays such as holding a piece of cotton on the end of a straw. The first finished was Frances Rabbit's gang. We had other relays, dances, and games.

The judges for our costumes were Miss Higgins and Miss Crow Shoe. The winners were Helen Weasel Bear, first prize 75 cents; Roderick North Peigan, second prize 50 cents; and Sharon Crow Shoe, third prize 25 cents. We paraded in a circle while we were being judged.

Some boys and girls cut pumpkin faces out of apples. Then the lights went out and a ghost came in and frightened us.

We had apples and jelly beans before we went to bed.

HALLOWE'EN PARTY by Mildred Woodman, grade 4

as taken from St. Cyprian's Newsletter, November, 1956

Last Wednesday we had a Hallowe'en party. It was the last day of October.

We had early supper. We didn't go up to the chapel. We went up to our playroom.

The boys gathered the dishes, and I was one of the dining room girls. I had to go in and help wipe the dishes. When we came out, we got dressed up. Ada was in the hospital so she didn't have Hallowe'en with us. She just came back last Thursday.

WINTER IS COMING:

Children Sliding by Gordon Buffalo, grade 2B

THE W.A., G.A., JA., and so on . . .

by Laura Stanger, 2012

Within the pages of this book a reader will learn that student and staff members enjoyed reporting their group activities in the W.A., G.A., J.A., C.B.L., J.B.L., and Little Helpers. Because those initials frequently appear in those reports, the following explains what they mean, and tells something about their development and focus.

History: The Anglican Church Women in Canada have celebrated more than 125 years of formal missionary work. It was 1885 when several women went to Ottawa to meet with officials of the *Domestic and Foreign Missionary Society*. They were there to discuss forming an organization for women that would focus on supporting and augmenting the missionary work of the clergy.

They were given permission to form the *Women's Auxiliary of the Missionary Society of the Church of England in Canada* (W.A.) and soon their first official board was set up complete with a motto and an official hymn.

Soon W.A. branches began to spring up all across Canada. Yearly conferences were held and executive members changed at regular intervals. They raised money, made bales and sent them off to wherever they were needed. They bought vans and supported the van workers who took Sunday school, medical care, and social services into remote areas.

In western Canada, it seems to me that Jean Pinkham - wife of the Reverend Cyprian Pinkham and a sister-in-law of Colonel James Macleod, NWMP - was first president of the Calgary Diocesan Women's Auxiliary. She held the position from 1891 - 1904. Jean Pinkham was also founder and president of Calgary's Women's Hospital Aid Society. And in 1935 she received an Order of the British Empire for her community work.

Soon after the W.A. was organized, its members realized the importance of developing groups suitable for children, as those young people would become the future missionary workers. Those groups became known as **G.A.** (*Girls' Auxiliary*), **J.A.** (*Junior Girls' Auxiliary*), and **Little Helpers** (*for the youngest children*). Then came groups for boys. **C.B.L.** (*Church Boys' League*), and **J.B.L.** (*Junior Boys' League*).

The missionary ministry carried on by the W.A. (*Women's Auxiliary*) over the years is legendary and in 1966 the W.A. became the foundation for an expanded organization known as **A.C.W.** (*Anglican Church Women*).

As you continue to read our St. Cyprian's Newsletters, you will see how those organizations - and others - made it possible for us to provide not only home and school and church for the children in residence, but also to give them a vital sense of community as well.

OUR G.A. by Evelyn Crazy Boy, grade 8
as taken from St. Cyprian's Newsletter, December, 1956

We have our meetings in the staff sitting room every Thursday.

We have elected our officers for this year. The president is Frances Rabbit, and I am the secretary.

At each meeting we go to the chapel and Frances takes the worship service. We sing our G.A. hymn, and say our prayer, and then we go to the sitting room.

I read the minutes of the last meeting and we have two of the girls move that they are correct.

We take our sewing out. We are working on our Christmas project of making dolls' clothes. Then we have a few games, such as, "Grandmother's Fruit Basket Upset."

At the last meeting, we had a pencil and paper and Miss Higgins, our leader, switched off the lights. We had to draw a picture of a house, a tree with a bird in it, a fence and a trail leading from the house. In the dark! Frances and Betty Ann had the best pictures. They won autograph books.

We had our refreshments and then we closed with our closing song and taps.

OUR J.A. by Mildred Woodman, grade 4
as taken from St. Cyprian's Newsletter, December, 1956

We have J.A. on Wednesdays after school. To open our meeting, we go out in the hall, and two of the girls make an arch and we go under it and say the password. Then we sing a hymn and say our pledge to Mrs. Ellis.

We get into two teams and play a game. The side that wins gets a treat. One of the games is "Call The Chickens Home." The game comes from China. We have a story too.

The girls have new green ties. The big girls help the little girls to pass their pledges. Judy and myself have earned stripes.

We sing our closing song and say goodnight.

CHRISTMAS NOTICES FROM YOUR PASTOR

TO ALL FAMILIES AND FRIENDS OF ST. CYPRIAN'S:

You are invited to visit your children's classrooms:

The pupils of St. Cyprian's invite you to visit their classrooms while they are decorated for Christmas. You are welcome to drop in either Friday December 14 or Sunday December 16.

Our Christmas concert will be in the community hall in Brocket on Thursday December 20 at 7:30 p.m. Everyone is welcome.

Christmas holidays:

Our residential school children will be free to go home on Friday December 21 at 4 o'clock.

The time to return to school will be Wednesday January 2 during the afternoon.

MERRY CHRISTMAS!   HAPPY NEW YEAR!

On behalf of my family and all of the staff here at St. Cyprian's, our best wishes to each of you at Christmas, and may the New Year be filled with blessings. As God gives us life, may we use each day under His guidance.

Star over Bethlehem by Arnold Crazy Boy, grade 8

RADIO BROADCAST, by Woodrow North Peigan, grade 5, as taken from St. Cyprian's Newsletter, January, 1957

Every second Wednesday afternoon, on the School Broadcast on the radio, there is a program on drawing. Usually they tell a story and play music that goes with the story. Then they ask the children to draw the picture that they see while listening. I drew soldiers marching the day we listened to march music.

LASSIE - a book report by Joe Crow Shoe Jr., grade 6
as taken from St. Cyprian's Newsletter, January, 1957

Our teacher has just finished reading us a story called, "Lassie Come Home."

Lassie was a dog owned by Joe Carraclough, who lived at Greenall Bridge. Every afternoon at four o'clock Lassie would wait for Joe at the school gate.

One day Joe's father lost his job and Lassie had to be sold. She was sold to the Duke of Rudling, but she ran away twice, and waited for Joe at the school gate.

Later, the Duke took Lassie to Northern Scotland, four hundred miles north of Greenall Bridge. Lassie escaped from there and started for the south again. On her way home, she was captured by dog catchers, and escaped from them.

On and on and on Lassie went. She met a pedlar named Rowlie and travelled part of the way with him.

One day, a funny thing happened. Lassie was again waiting for Joe at the school gate, nearly dead. Mr. and Mrs. Carraclough saved Lassie.

In the end, the Duke hired Joe's father and they all went to live on the Duke's estate where they were very happy again.

Lassie by Joe Crow, grade 6

SMILE

Old friend: "Where have you been for the past few years?"
Student: "At college taking medicine."
Old Friend: "I'm sorry to hear that. How do you feel now?"

THIS AND THAT by Elizabeth Crow Flagg, grade 8
as taken from St. Cyprian's Newsletter, January, 1957

All the boys and girls except the grade one children went skating on Monday night. We all enjoyed ourselves. The girls skated at one end of the rink and the boys practiced hockey at the other.

Wednesday night, our hockey team played against a Pincher Creek team. The girls went along to cheer for our team, but we didn't do much good. The score was 3-1 for Pincher Creek.

Judy and John Stanger's grandparents, Mr. and Mrs. Harris, are visiting here from Ontario. They arrived in time for Christmas and are driving back through the southern states. Mrs. Wilson, Judy's and John's great aunt from Quebec also visited for a few days and is driving back with Mr. and Mrs. Harris.

Walter Crow Shoe has a new baby sister. Her name is Joanne Marie.

Caroline and Kenneth Yellow Horn have a new sister named Lenora.

Over the Christmas holidays, I cut my foot on a saw. It got infected so I had to see the doctor several times. It's all better now, just in time to be able to go skating.

Mr. Buchanan of Edgerton, Alberta, is now working here. He has taken Mr. Irwin's place as farmer.

George Crow Shoe's brother, Claire, had his back hurt and spent some time in the hospital. He is much better now and is back at home.

The boys and girls would like to express their thanks to all the staff who helped make their 1956 Christmas so nice. The girls especially want to say thank you to Mrs. Ellis for the record player and sled which she gave us. The boys are very happy with the construction camp which Miss Bray gave them, and they also say thank you.

Miss How has a new pupil. He is Leroy Black Eyes.

The Guides are starting to work on their cooking badges. Mrs. Stanger gives us lessons on Thursday nights. We enjoy them.

The J.A. girls are looking very smart these days in their dark green skirts, white blouses, green ties, and brand new green beanies which were made for them since our last paper. Annabelle Buffalo and Evelina Iron Shirt now have their first stripes.

To earn the first stripe a J.A. member has to know: The J.A. Promise, Motto, Aim, Member's Prayer, and learn a game from other lands.

WINTER FUN by Mildred Woodman, grade 4

as taken from St. Cyprian's Newsletter, February, 1957

Most of all, what I like is skating, because it is fun. Pincher Creek is so big, that's why I like to go there.

Next comes sliding. Sliding is fun too. When I'm home I go sliding down by the spring. There is a great big snowbank there, and we slide down it.

Next comes hockey. The boys like to play hockey but hockey isn't for girls, yet. It is for boys. The girls just go and cheer for their school. Our boys have won twice when they played against the R.C. school boys.

Next is playing games. We play tag in the snow and we play follow the leader. Then we play snowballs. It's fun playing snowball.

That's all I can think of just now.

SQUARE DANCING by Joe Crow Shoe, grade 6
as taken from St. Cyprian's Newsletter, February, 1957

On Tuesday night we went down to the square dancing at the hall. Mr. Stanger drove us down. We will be going every Monday night.

We danced some round dances. It was a lot of fun learning all the new dances. They were Jolly Is The Miller Who Lives By The Mill, Oh Johnny, and a square dance called Red Wing or Dip and Dive. I enjoyed them very much. It was lots of fun.

THIS AND THAT by Evelyn Crazy Boy, grade 8
as taken from St. Cyprian's Newsletter, March - April, 1957

Several of our children and staff have been sick in bed with colds and flu, but are up again, feeling much better. Mrs. Stanger took the place of Miss Koski, our teacher, in the senior classroom for a couple of days when Miss Koski was sick in bed with a cold.

Mr. Irwin dropped in to say hello one day last week. He was on his way for a visit in Winnipeg.

Clarence and Alfreda Knowlton are now the proud parents of a baby girl. Congratulations.

The girls saw a gopher while taking a walk the end of February after a Chinook had arrived and made the temperature climb from ten degree below zero all the way up to forty-one degrees above zero. So we went from digging our way through the snow one day to wading through mud and water the next!

March came in like a lamb, and in this spot we had a very nice day. The sun shone, there was very little wind and the temperature was forty-five degrees. Then March went out like a lion. The morning of April 1, 1957, when we got up, we weren't too surprised to see the ground again white with snow.

We wish to extend our sympathy to Helen, Butch, and Hazel Weasel Bear whose grandmother, Mrs. Coldweather, passed away recently.

Mr. Stanger mentioned today that there has been an average of two baptisms a month since September. Congratulation to all these folks this month:

    Archie and Nancy Big Swan, a boy, Archie David

    Roy and Beatrice Big Bull, a son, Rodney Dean

    Isabelle Morning Bull, a daughter, Lorraine

    Sam and Ruth Good Rider, a daughter, Gayleen May

    Robert and Hazel North Peigan, a son, Eldon Gordon

    Mrs. David Crow Shoe, a daughter, Coleen Brenda

    (Frances Rabbit and Evelyn Crazy Boy chose Coleen Brenda's name, and are her godmothers.)

Mervyn and Jessie Crow Shoe, two of our former pupils, left last Friday for Prince Albert, where they are attending a three-week course.

Mr. Buchanan, who has been working here this winter, left today to return to his home. Mr. Brown has gone back to working days.

Two new pupils started school this week. They are Conrad and Sandra Big Bull.

Sunday nights after Sunday School, the girls are having singsongs. Miss Higgins and Mrs. Ellis lead them, and there are refreshments after.

Little Ada Buffalo has been ill with tonsillitis.

Eric Crow Shoe banged his thumb one day when he fell, and is going to lose the nail.

Delma Crow Shoe tumbled off a see-saw and gave herself a black eye.

SPECIAL NOTICE: Easter Holidays - Children may go home Thursday, April 18 at 2 p.m. and are asked to return on Sunday, April 28 at 2 p.m.

W.A. NOTES by Miss Bray
as taken from St. Cyprian's Newsletter, March - April, 1957

The Peigan W.A. will meet on Wed. April 10 at 2: p.m. at the Community Hall. A report of the Diocesan Annual Meeting in Calgary will be given.

The Fort Macleod Deanery Meeting will be held in Blairmore on April 30. We hope the Peigan W.A. ladies will turn out for this session. Transportation will be arranged.

There is a total of 104 Little Helpers enrolled now. Member's cards will be given out to the new members shortly.

G.A. NOTES by Agnes Strikes With A Gun, grade 6
as taken from St. Cyprian's Newsletter, March - April, 1957

We still have G.A. on Thursday nights. We start our meetings with a little service in the chapel, and then we come into our classroom to study more about cooking, with Mrs. Stanger.

Several weeks ago, Mrs. Stanger took us down to her kitchen to cook eggs. They were fried, scrambled, and boiled. Five girls went down first and then the second group went. After the eggs were cooked, we ate them. We enjoyed that.

We are also making felt bookmarks for our prayer books. Several of the girls have started, but I haven't started mine. We're also making belts for our uniforms and hooking rugs. We've finished two, one with a flower and one with a beaver. Right now we're doing a rug with ducks on it.

ST. CYPRIAN'S STAFF
as recorded in St. Cyprian's Newsletter dated May-June, 1957

THE REVEREND AND MRS. STANGER and their children, Judith and John, came to us from Chooutla Residential School, Carcross, Yukon. Mr. Stanger is a graduate of St. John's College, Winnipeg, Manitoba, and came here as principal last summer. Mr. Stanger's hometown is Edmonton, Alberta; Mrs. Stanger's is Shawville, Quebec. Judith was born in Whitehorse, Yukon, and John in Pembroke, Ontario. Both attend school here.

MISS LORRAINE HIGGINS: Her hometown is St. John, New Brunswick. She is a graduate of the Anglican Women's Training College in Toronto. She came to us by way of Sioux Lookout, Ontario, and Chapleau, Quebec. She has been matron here for four years.

MISS ELSIE BRAY is from Medicine Hat, Alberta, but she has been here since 1943 as the boys' supervisor. She is also very active on the reserve with the W.A., and her Little Helpers group has an enrollment of over one hundred pre-school children.

MRS. EDITH ELLIS comes from Brantford, Ontario. She was new to the Indian School system when she came here two years ago. She is the girls' supervisor, and leader of our J.A. group.

MISS EVELYN CROW SHOE is a graduate of this school, and her home is in Brocket, Alberta - right here on the Peigan Reserve. She is the staff relief supervisor, and has spent two summers attending leadership and recreational courses at Red Deer. She also teaches dancing, games, etc. to the children.

MRS. MARY FIDLER comes from Mount Nebo, Saskatchewan. She came here via Alert Bay, Prince Albert, and Sioux Lookout. She has been doing the cooking here for the past three years.

MISS ETHEL BAYNE is from Brandon, Manitoba. She came here with seven years experience in Indian schools at Moose Fort, Shingwauk, Sioux Lookout, and Birtle. She has been general assistant here for the past year.

MR. ANDREW BROWN (Andy to most of us): He first arrived in Canada from Scotland in 1912. He has lived in the Pincher Creek area since 1920, and has worked here for almost five years as night watchman, and he also does general maintenance in and around the building which includes the lawn and gardens.

MR. JOHN IRWIN has been the school's farmer for more than 20 years.

MISS KATHLEEN HOW: Her hometown is Vancouver, but she has been with Indian schools for fifteen years, and at this school for three. She teaches the primary classes. She is the only staff member to own a car and likes to quote one of the boys who says, "She drags us around."

MISS JEAN KOSKI: Her hometown is Athelstan, Quebec, but she came west six years ago, and was a supervisor at Gleichen and Morley for four years. She teaches the senior pupils.

A SMILE FROM THE SENIOR CLASSROOM

The dentist was here recently and did everyone's teeth. When it was time for the pupils in Miss Koski's classroom to go to get their teeth checked, this is what happened:

Miss Koski: "Who would like to . . .

Sam: "Me, me!"

Miss Koski: . . . be first to go to the dentist?"

Sammy went first, not too willingly, but he came back happy. He needed nothing done.

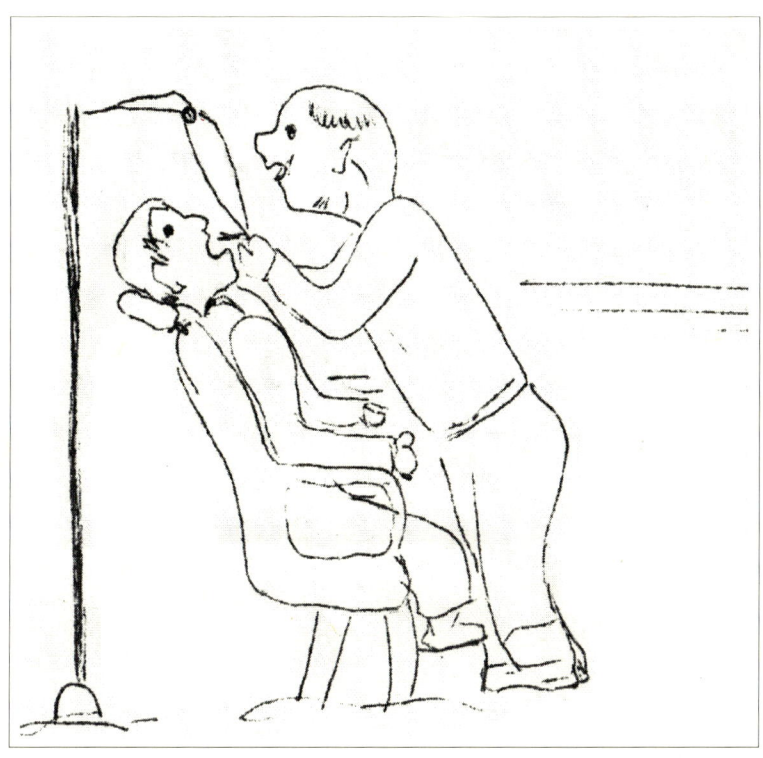

J.A. RALLY
as taken from St. Cyprian's Newsletter, May-June, 1957

Mrs. Ellis and Miss How took seven of the J.A. girls to the J.A. Rally at Christ Church in Fort Macleod on Saturday, May 25. All the children attended a church service. Then they played games and each group took part in the program. Our girls sang "Jesus Loves Me" in Blackfoot. Mildred and Patsy were in Indian dress and the others wore their uniforms.

CADET SCHEME by George Crow Shoe, grade 8
as taken from St. Cyprian' Newsletter, May-June, 1957

On May 3, we went on a scheme in High Bush with the Pincher Creek Cadet Corps. We took our blankets because we were going to sleep down there. First, we all met at the Community Hall in

Brocket. Then we marched down to the river bottom while our instructors rode in the truck.

When we got to the place where we were going, we were divided into two groups, Pincher Creek on one side and Brocket on the other. The Pincher Creek boys made a fire quite a distance away from us while we made our fire not far from where we had supper. We put up a radio at each campfire and talked over them.

When it was dark, some of the cadets from each camp went on patrol while some of the others stood guard around each campfire in case the others tried to capture it. I was one of the guards there, and Roderick was operating the radio for our campfire. About midnight it started to rain and we all had to get into the army truck and go up to the Community Hall and sleep there. The floor was so hard that I twisted and turned nearly all night. In the morning we went back down to the river bottom and had breakfast. When we finished, we all went home.

GIRLS' AUXILIARY FESTIVAL by Evelyn Crazy Boy, grade 8
as taken from St. Cyprian's Newsletter, May-June, 1957

On Saturday morning May 11, at eight o'clock, we left the school to go to the festival in Calgary. Mr. Stanger took the girls and Miss Higgins in the school station wagon. Our first stop was at Claresholme where we went into a restaurant and each had a bottle of pop and rested a little while. We stopped again at High River for fresh air and to take some pictures.

We got to Paget Hall in Calgary just in time to have our lunch in the dining room with the other girls who were there ahead of us.

They were from Calgary, Lethbridge, Olds, and Carbon. After lunch, we went upstairs and got seats. The meeting opened with the GA hymn and prayers. The secretary of each group read reports of their year's work. After I read mine, a lady made a speech about a camp that would be at Waterton Park this summer. Some plays were put on by different groups of girls. The part I liked best was the fashion show.

At five o'clock we all went downstairs to the dining room for the banquet. We didn't have time to stay for the service at the Cathedral. We arrived home at ten-thirty, all very sleepy and tired.

SMILES

- A little girl asked her supervisor, Mrs. Ellis, if she could go to see Mikey Mouse on TV.

    Mrs. Ellis insisted that she meant Mickey Mouse, but both were wrong! The program was Mighty Mouse.

- Another little girl, sitting on the teeter-toter with the sun in her eyes, said, "Look, I'm locking my eyes."

THE GRADE EIGHT GRADUATES

(as taken from St. Cyprian's Newsletter dated June, 1957)

Elizabeth Rosaline Crow Flagg (Liz)

Ambition: hairdresser

Favorite Pastime: threading necklaces

Favorite Expression: It's too hard!

Pet Hate: social studies

Extra Activities: G.A., cooking, home nursing, churchmanship, mission study, handicrafts, Bible study, choir, square dance club

We predict: Elizabeth will make a living making beaded headdresses.

Evelyn Sylvia Crazy Boy (Lyn)

Ambition: salesgirl

Favorite Pastime: writing letters when she is supposed to be studying

Favorite expression: Am I going to pass this year?

Pet Hate: hearing "E-v-e-l-y-n!"

Extra Activities: G.A. cooking, home nursing, mission study, handicraft badges, choir, square dance club

We predict that Evelyn will make her living selling Elizabeth's beaded headdresses.

George Stanley Crow Shoe (Kid)

Ambition: engineer

Favorite Pastime: rewriting science notes

Favorite Expression: That'll be the day!

Pet Hate: coming anywhere in his class but first

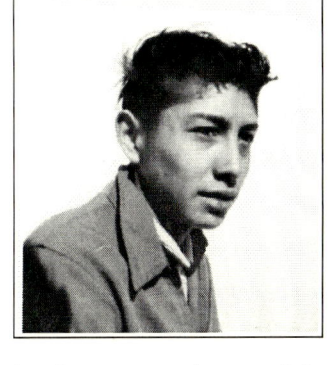

Extra Activities: cadets (lance bombardier), square dance club, handicrafts, choir, softball, hockey

We predict that George will be the first of the class to get married.

Wayne Stanley Knowlton (Weiners)

Ambition: mechanic

Favorite Pastime: teasing the girls

Favorite Expression: Gee whizzes

Pet Hate: girls (???)

Extra Activities: cadets (bombardier), choir, handicrafts, softball, hockey

Our congratulations to Wayne; on May 29 he received an award as best cadet in the Peigan Cadet Corp, Camp Vernon, B.C.

We predict that Wayne will be official garageman for St. Cyprian's broken down toy car department.

Roderick North Peigan

Ambition: army

Favorite Pastime: quarreling with the girls

Favorite Expression: Hi-i-yuh! (Blackfoot for anything from 'Oh yeah!' to 'Try and make me!')

Pet Hate: school, school, school

Extra Activities: cadets, square dance club, handicrafts, choir, hockey, softball

We predict that Roderick will spend a lot of his time wishing he were back in school.

Miss Jean Koski, senior classroom teacher, says that Elizabeth, Evelyn, Wayne and Roderick will be taking their grade nine at St. Paul's School, Cardston. George will be going to Pincher Creek.

Cowboy riding by Joe Crow Shoe, grade 6

CHAPTER FIVE

SCHOOL TERM: 1957 - 1958

ST. CYPRIAN'S RESIDENTIAL SCHOOL PUPILS - SEPTEMBER, 1957

as taken from The Anglican Newsletter dated September, 1957

Kindergarten	Grade One	Grade Two
Sandra Big Bull	Conrad Big Bull	Woodrow Crow Eagle
Ada Buffalo	Leroy Black Eyes	Donna Crow Shoe
Loretta Crow Eagle	Melinda Crow Eagle	Glennis Crow Shoe
Florence Weasel Bear	Darryl Crow Shoe	Diane North Peigan
Reggie Crow Shoe	Eric Crow Shoe	Linda North Peigan
Vernon Morning Bull	Aloise Iron Shirt	Harvey Plain Eagle
Melvin Plain Eagle	Hazel Crazy Boy	Corinne Iron Shirt
Eric North Peigan	Louis Crow Eagle	Doreen Weasel Bear
	Oliver Crow Eagle	Gordon Buffalo
	Valerie Crow Shoe	Barbara Ann Crow Shoe
	Linda Yellow Horn	Louisa Crow Shoe
		Robert Crow Shoe
		Ruby Crow Shoe
		Roberta Iron Shirt
		Billy North Peigan

Grade Three	Grade Four	Grade Five
Mary Born With A Tooth Gerald Crazy Boy Gerald Crow Shoe Melvin Iron Shirt Caroline Yellow Horn John Stanger Betty Red Young Man	Kenneth Yellow Horn Patsy Yellow Horn Clifford Crow Shoe Walter Crow Shoe Sandra North Peigan Delma Crow Shoe	Ronnie Morning Bull Sammy Born With A Tooth Mildred Woodman Hazel Weasel Bear Vera North Peigan Annabelle Buffalo Judith Stanger

Grade Six	Grade Seven	Grade Eight
Woodrow North Peigan Eileen North Peigan	Agnes Strikes With A Gun Betty Ann Crow Shoe Sharon Crow Shoe Helen Weasel Bear Joe Crow Shoe George (Butch) Weasel Bear Arnold Crazy Boy	nil

Total Pupils: 63   boys: 29   girls: 34 - one-quarter of total named Crow Shoe

Junior Classroom: 41 pupils in beginners to end of grade three. Teacher: Miss How

Senior Classroom: 22 pupils, in grade four to end of grade seven. Teacher: Miss Mason

GENERAL SCHOOL ROUTINE - MONDAY THROUGH FRIDAY

    6:30   Rising bell
    7:30   Breakfast, followed by chores
    9:00   Chapel Assembly, with children going directly to classes until noon

Morning recess 10:30 to 10:45

    12:15   Dinner, followed by chores and play outdoors
    1:30   Classes until 4:00 p.m.

Afternoon recess 2:45 to 3:00

    4:15   Sports, walks, group meetings, etc.
    6:00   Supper, free play, planned activities, etc.
    7:30   Junior bedtime
    8:30   Senior bedtime

Friday afternoon, after classes, parents may take their children home for the weekend, but they must be back by 2 p.m. Sunday.

Sunday evening, Sunday School, for all, 6:30 p.m.

SCHEDULE OF WEEKDAY ACTIVITIES:

MONDAY
    Volleyball (when weather permits) after 4 p.m.
    Singsong, for all, 6:30 - 7:00
    Senior Sewing Class 7:30 - 8:30, with Miss Higgins

TUESDAY
    Junior Sewing Classes, with Miss Bayne and Mrs. Stanger 4:15 - 5:15
    G.A. with Miss Higgins 7:30 - 8:30

WEDNESDAY
  4:15 - 5:15
  Sunbeam Club, with Miss Bayne
  J.A., with Mrs. Ellis
  Junior Boys' League, with Miss Crow Shoe
  Church Boys' League, with Mrs. Stanger

THURSDAY
  Volleyball, when weather permits
  Choir Practice 7:15 - 8:00, with Miss Higgins

In addition: - Leathercraft, with Miss Bray, for both boys and girls.

Television may be watched at such times as children cannot play outdoors, aren't otherwise occupied, and the program is suitable for children.

Piano lessons, with Mrs. Stanger, Friday after school, present pupils are Mildred Woodman, Gerald Crazy Boy, as well as Judy and John Stanger.

PARISH AND SCHOOL NEWS, from your clergyman and principal, Rev. Stanger, for The Anglican Newsletter of St. Cyprian's School and St. Cyprian's Church

Church Services are held in St. Cyprian's Church, Brocket, each Sunday afternoon at 3 o'clock.

Holy Communion is on the first Sunday of each month and at special seasons as announced.

Sunday, October 6, will be our Harvest Thanksgiving service with Holy Communion

Sunday, October 20, is set aside as Children and Youth Sunday.

Sunday School is held at St. Cyprian's School
- Beginners to the end of grade two meet in the larger classroom with Miss Higgins, Miss Bayne, and Miss Crow Shoe.
- Miss How has the grade three pupils.
- Mrs. Ellis has the grade four pupils.
- Miss Mason has the grades five and six pupils.
- Mrs. Fiddler is the organist for the Sunday School before they all break-off to go to their classes.

Choir
- Our school choir consists of nine boys and eight girls. The aim is to sing with spirit, and learn the meaning behind some of the hymns.

Baptisms
- Malcolm James, son of Jerry and Rose Potts
- Marcia Ann, daughter of Laura White Cow
- Gregory Blair, son of Gladys Baptiste
- Sam Bernard James, son of Edward and Eleanor Warrior
- Stanford Grand, son of Margaret and Jim Plain Eagle

Burials
- David Crow Shoe
- Brenda Colleen Crow Shoe

BEST WISHES
- to Mrs. Raymond Bad Eagle, formerly Eva Yellow Horn, and graduate of St. Cyprian's School

She has given birth to triplets, three girls, born in Pincher Creek Hospital on September 26.

- to the following former pupils of St. Cyprian's School:
- Melvin Crow Shoe, George Crow Shoe, Wayne Knowlton, Melvin Potts, Peter Yellow Horn

These young men are going by bus to Pincher Creek High School

- to Lewis Strikes With A Gun, Roderick North Peigan, Elizabeth Crow Flagg, and Evelyn Crazy Boy

These young people are residing at St. Paul's I.R.S., and going to Cardston High School.

PARISH MEETINGS, by Miss Bray, as reported in The Anglican Newsletter, Thanksgiving, 1957

The Peigan W.A. started the new term with a meeting at the home of Bessie North Peigan. There were ten members present. Sewing and embroidery work was given out. At the next meeting movies will be shown at the Community Hall, date to be set later.

The Little Helpers Annual Party is set for October 31. It will be with Miss Bray in the Community Hall. There are 104 Little Helpers on the Roll Call at the present time.

IF WISHES COULD COME TRUE
as taken from The Anglican Newsletter, Thanksgiving, 1957

by Butch Weasel Bear, grade 7

I wish I was an elephant, so huge and so strong that I could boss all the other animals. To be king of the jungle! But one animal I could not boss, so big and strong, is the lion that roars so loudly that he frightens the small animals.

by Betty Ann Crow Shoe, grade 7

I wish to be a teacher so that I can get enough money to travel around and go to different places to teach Indian pupils.

by Agnes Strikes With A Gun, grade 7

I wish to see Elvis Presley in person. Why? Because I've seen him on TV and from his beautiful singing and photograph, I want to see him.

by Mildred Woodman, grade 5

I'd wish for a little nightingale to sing to me and to sing me to sleep.

by Patsy Yellow Horn, grade 4

I'd wish for the most beautiful thing in the world, a pony to ride on every day at home.

by Sammy Born With A Tooth, grade 5

I'd wish for a horse, a BB gun, and a house all my own.

SMILE

Betty was slouched over her desk and her feet were out in the aisle. Besides that, she was noisily chewing gum.

The teacher said, "Betty! Take the gum out of your mouth and put your feet in!"

SINGSONGS by Agnes Strikes With A Gun, grade 7
as taken from The Anglican Newsletter, Thanksgiving, 1957

We have singing in the junior classroom every Monday night. We have choruses and hymns, rounds and songs. Mrs. Stanger plays the piano for us, and Miss Higgins leads the singing. We are very pleased that Mildred Woodman (grade five) can play some of the songs for us. And we sure enjoy singing!

INSIDE FUN

Some boys are busy making wire horses and cowboys. Corrals will be made later - all miniature in size, but very lifelike.

The girls have a game on their day-room floor. Two checker boards have been designed in the tiles. Soon the CBL boys will have finished wooden blocks in blue and red so we can play during the winter.

OUTSIDE FUN

The boys and girls are enjoying volleyball twice a week under the leadership of Miss Higgins and Miss Crow Shoe. Mr. Brown made the court in the girls' play yard, and Mr. Doolittle made a very fine score-keeper from plywood. We have four teams. So far the champions are The Indian Head Rockets, the boys' team, which is coached by Miss Crow Shoe. But coach Higgins is still in there pitching, she says her girls will win soon.

OTHER NEWS AT THE SCHOOL:

First, two new staff members: Miss Mason, the teacher for the senior classroom, and Mr. Doolittle, our nightwatchman.

Mr. Andrew Brown is on holidays somewhere in Alberta.

The halls in the school all have new linoleum laid since last term. Also in the girls' playroom. Much painting was done during the summer holidays too. Thanks to staff members.

Two little girls, Florence Weasel Bear and Loretta Crow Eagle have come to school for the first time. And on the boys' side, Reggie Crow Shoe, Vernon Morning Bull, Melvin Plain Eagle, and Eric North Peigan.

Staff members interested in forming a **St. Cyprian's school branch of the Women's Auxiliary,** recently met in the

Stanger's apartment. Our membership is seven. Two of the staff members are also members in the Peigan Reserve W.A. Our meetings are being held every second Saturday at 8:45 p.m. As our first project, it was decided that each of the members knit or sew something suitable for the Baptismal Bundles For Babies. Because our W.A. funds are nil, each member offered to buy the necessary materials for her contribution. Although a comparatively small group, we hope to be able to accomplish much, both spiritually and materially.

BOYS AND GIRLS:

HALLOWE'EN is just around the corner! You better soon get busy working on those costumes.

CHRISTMAS, 1957

NOTES FROM YOUR CLERGYMAN AND PRINCIPAL
as printed in The Anglican Newsletter, Christmas edition

Christmas Services at St. Cyprian's Church, Brocket, Alberta:

- A Carol Service will be held at 3 p.m. on December 15.
- Christmas Communion, at 3 p.m. Christmas Day.

Recent Burial:

Since or last newsletter there has been one burial, that of Hazel Yellow Face, daughter of Sam and Agnes Yellow Face.

Anglican Sunday School of the Air:

Each Sunday morning at 9 o'clock, over radio station CFCN Calgary, an Anglican Church in the Diocese of Calgary broadcasts its *Sunday School of the Air*.

On Sunday, December 22, Indian Schools and Missions will be especially remembered in the churches of our diocese as appointed in the Prayer Calendar.

Christmas Tree Scene, grade 2

NOTICE TO ALL PARENTS OF PUPILS AT ST. CYPRIAN'S SCHOOL:

St. Cyprian's School Christmas Concert: Tuesday December 17 at 8 p.m. in the Brocket Community Hall.

Christmas Holidays: Pupils in residence will be ready to go home for their holidays at 4 p.m. on Friday, December 20. They are asked to return to school on Sunday, January 5 by 2 p.m.

A BRIGHT BEAUTIFUL STAR
as taken from the Christmas, 1957 edition of The Anglican Newsletter

Long, long ago some wise men - looking at the stars one night noticed something was different. "Look," said one of the men, "look, way up there. High above our heads is a very bright beautiful new star. Isn't that strange?"

As the men gazed at the new star it began to move across the sky. "Perhaps we should follow it," said one of them. "Come," said another, "we must follow it. I think it will lead us to the King."

All night they followed the star. When it was day, they could not see the star, so they rested.

When it was dark again they watched the sky. The bright star was still there, and again it began to move across the sky. "We must follow it again tonight," they agreed.

All that night, and for many more nights, they followed the bright beautiful star. Then one morning, they came to a city. "Maybe we will find the King in this big city," said one of the wise men.

All day they looked and looked for the King. They asked people in the city where to find Him, but no one knew anything about a King being there. So, again, they waited for night.

There it was! The special star was still up there. Again, it began to move. Again, they followed it. Suddenly, it stopped. The star stopped moving directly over a stable. "Why would the King be in a stable?" they wondered.

Well, when the three wise men looked in, what they saw was a little baby sleeping in a manger. It was the little baby Jesus. And Mary his mother was watching over Him.

The wise men were very glad that they had followed the bright beautiful star all the way to the baby Jesus. They gave Him gifts. They worshipped Him. They thanked God for the star that had guided them all the way to their newborn King.

PARISH NEWS, reported by Miss Bray

taken from The Anglican Newsletter, Christmas, 1957

The Brocket Whirlaway Square Dance Club started again on November 4 with a very good turn out. Officers for the coming year are: President, Joe Crow Shoe; Vice-president, Clare Crow Shoe; Secretary-Treasurer, Evelyn Crow Shoe. There will be square dances every Monday night in the Community Hall.

The Peigan W.A. had a very successful sale of their work - aprons, quilts, and dresses. There was also a Rummage Sale on Nov. 21. The Christmas meeting and party will be on Tuesday, December 10 at the hall.

The Annual Little Helpers' party was held in the Community Hall on November 26. There was a good turn out - 55 little ones and 30 mothers. After a short service, a few games were played. Lunch was served and gifts were given to the children. Some mothers came who couldn't bring their little ones, so bags of cookies, candies and gifts were sent to them. Miss Evelyn Crow Shoe assisted Miss Bray. Thanks go out to all who helped make this party a success.

WHAT'S NEW?

We have one new boy. He is in Kindergarten, and he just loves to sharpen pencils! Who is he? Melvin Douglas Yellow Horn, of course.

The total of residential pupils is now 62. Twenty-nine boys and thirty-three girls.

Agnes Strikes With A Gun is busy making a purse. Sharon Crow Shoe has finished hers. The senior boys are making belts for themselves now. Some boys and girls are making change purses.

The Senior Sewing Class has changed its meeting to Wednesday evenings.

The boys and girls may go to their homes every second weekend now. On Sunday when they are at school, we have Morning Prayer Service in the chapel. The alternate Sunday there is Holy Communion for the staff.

SPECIAL THANKS:

Donations have been sent to us to help the children at the school, the little ones on the reserve, and the parents.

Our sincere thanks to groups and individuals in the following places: Pincher Creek, Calgary, Nova Scotia, Hobbema, Gleichen, Medicine Hat, Oliver, Empress, Brantford, Saskatoon, Ashton, Chilliwack, Victoria, London, Glanworth, Drummondville, and Regina.

SMILES:

- Oliver, brushing his teeth vigorously, says, "Look, I'm brushing hard so my teeth will be golden white!"

  . . .

- While several children were in bed sick recently, we found out we have the makings of one really good nurse. Using her toothbrush as a thermometer, shaking it down conscientiously, she kept check on the temperature of her dolly.

  . . .

- Another little girl has added something to the duties of supervisors. She asked her supervisor to keep watch over a snowman for her, "So the boys won't knock it down."

· · ·

- One J.A. girl said to Mrs. Ellis, "Shall I leave the honour roll up on the lantern?"   What she meant was the landing.

· · ·

- Two little boys playing I spy with my little eye:

    Louis: I spy something that begins with snow.
    Eric: I know. It's a cold day!

NOTES FROM GROUPS
as taken from The Anglican Newsletter dated December, 1957

Sewing Class by Patsy Yellow Horn, grade 4

Our sewing class meets every Tuesday at 4 o'clock. We learn sewing with the sewing machine. We made half-slips. I made a barber's cape. Sandra and Delma made tea towels. After Christmas we are going to make a dress using a pattern.

Sewing Class by Judith Stanger, grade 5

Our sewing class has cut out some babies' dresses. The ones who can sew straight, will sew them up. We are going to make some half-slips when we all can sew well. In our spare time we crochet strings by hand for the little girls' mittens.

J.A. by Hazel Weasel Bear, grade 5

We have J.A. every Wednesday at 4 p.m. One week we have badge work and another we have activity. We sure enjoy playing games from other lands. In our activity we are making a Palestine house, and studying about their people. Some of us are making Christmas decorations for the girls' playroom.

G.A. by Helen Weasel Bear, grade 7

Our G.A. meetings are held each week in the staff sitting room. We open our meetings with a singsong. Then we repeat together the G.A. Promise. Then we have a short business meeting. Our worship service is in the chapel. We sing our G.A. hymn, and one girl reads from the Bible. We are learning to play Scrabble. After our game, we have refreshments. We close with prayer.

C.B.L. by Joe Crow Shoe - "Sir Joe" - grade 7

Since the last newsletter, twelve boys have become squires. To earn the title of squire, a member has to know the League Prayer, Aim, Motto, Purpose, Code, and The Lord's Prayer. He must go to Sunday School regularly. He must be able to hop 25 feet on one leg. In handicrafts we are making checker blocks, spool toys, plaques, doll cribs, etc.

SINGSONG by Mildred Woodman, grade 5

We have singsong Monday nights right after supper. We learn new songs, and also sing ones that we know. Sometimes Judy Stanger and I play the piano for the children. We all enjoy singsong.

ST. CYPRIAN'S CHRISTMAS CONCERT
Tuesday, December 17 - 8 p.m.
at the
Brocket Community Hall
The Program:

1) O Canada
2) Christmas Songs - Primary Girls
3) Skit - Going Driving - Senior Classroom
4) Ten Little Indians - Grades 2 & 3 Girls & the Primary Boys
5) Songs - The First Snowflake & The Toymaker's Dream - Seniors
6) Play - Grades Two and Three
7) Duet - The Lantern - Sammy Born With A Tooth & Sandra North Peigan

INTERMISSION

Candy, etc. will be on sale at intermission time

8) Choral Reading - Senior Classroom
9) Group Singing - Senior Classroom
10) Square Dance
11) Play - Christmas Shopping - Senior Classroom
12) Folk Dance - Grades 1 and 2
13) Pageant - Senior Classroom
14) Piano Selections - Mildred Woodman & Judy Stanger
15) The Queen

Please bring this program with you to the concert. We are trying to reserve seats for our pupils' parents and friends who have programs.

MERRY CHRISTMAS AND A HAPPY NEW YEAR FROM THE STAFF OF ST. CYPRIAN'S INDIAN RESIDENTIAL SCHOOL

L. Kathleen How, Noreen Mason, Laura M. Stanger, Evelyn Crowshoe, Marion Crowshoe, Edith Ellis, Mary Fidler, Elsie Bray, C T Stanger, C Doolittle, Andy Brown, Marie Crow Shoe, E. M. Bayne

OUR PURPOSE:

To do our utmost to train and educate the boys and girls of our school in the Christian Way of Life, and to prepare them, by academic instruction, to do their part to make their homes, their community, and their country, a better place in which to live.

ST. CYPRIAN'S INDIAN RESIDENTIAL SCHOOL
Peigan Reserve, Brocket, Alberta

Easter, 1958

Dear Friends,

    With the coming of the New Year, there came a change in the care of the church's work on the Peigan Reserve.

    For many years the Missionary Society has provided men and money to carry on the work with Indian people in Canada. Clergymen were appointed as principals of the Indian Residential

Schools and, in some cases, they were appointed missionaries to the area in which the schools were located - just as it has been here on the Peigan Reserve.

With the coming of 1958, provision for the work among Indian people was assumed by the Diocese of Calgary. As a result, the Peigan Reserve has been attached to Fort Macleod and Claresholm, while the Missionary Society will continue to provide for Residential School work.

After many years of preparation, by preaching and teaching, it would appear that the church on the Peigan has come of age to take a place with neighbouring communities. This brings with it the opportunity of further growth in the life of our church.

For many years the people on the Peigan have enjoyed the assistance of people all over Canada. Now you will have the opportunity of showing that this help has enabled you to assume your place with other church communities. When we were children, we needed the help of adult people. When we became adults, we began to share with other adults in contributing to the welfare of the life of all. You, as a congregation, may now begin to provide for your church life as an adult church community.

All over Canada we find groups of church people growing in the service of Christ. Many of these growing communities have the care and guidance of a clergyman or a church worker. However, some communities are not able to have a clergyman. There just aren't enough to go around. Thus, people in some places carry on without a trained worker. You are fortunate in having the Rev. Doyle to care for and guide your church life. It is for you to put forward the effort which, under his guidance, will bring you to adult participation in the life of the church.

God bless you all,

Rev. C. T. Stanger, Principal

Easter Day

Easter Day is coming
The best day of the year.
For Easter brings the Springtime
And flowers and birds appear.

Easter brings the bunny
With a basket for a nest
The nest is full of candy eggs
The eggs we like the best.

But it means more than bunnies
And flowers and birds again
For Jesus rose on Easter Day
To show God's love for men.

Grades 1, 2, 3.

printed by —
Roberta Iron Shirt

Miss How: Have you finished drawing your chicken?
Gerald: I have just its hoofs to do!

SPECIAL NOTICE TO ALL PARENTS OF PUPILS AT ST. CYPRIAN'S SCHOOL:

Pupils will be ready to go for their Easter holidays at 4 p.m. on Thursday, April 3. They will return to school on Sunday, April 13, by 2 p.m.

LOCAL NEWS
as taken from The Anglican Newsletter dated Easter, 1958

Joe Crow Shoe Sr., a sub-chief of the Peigan Indian tribe, was made an honorary member of the Lethbridge and District Old Timers Pemmican Club in December, 1957. The ceremony took place at the Annual Ball in the Civic Centre, Lethbridge. Mrs. Crow Shoe, Evelyn, and Mervyn accompanied Mr. Crow Shoe to the ball. They were guests at the Marquis Hotel while in the city.

The induction of Rev. E. Doyle took place at Christ Church in Fort Macleod, February, 1958. Bishop Calvert and Archdeacon Axon officiated. A reception followed in the Parish Hall. Rev. Stanger, Chief John Yellow Horn, Sub-Chief Joe Crow Shoe, and Mr. Pete Potts were guests there from the Peigan Reserve.

The Wedding of Delores Scott and Andrew Creighton took place on the Peigan Reserve, January 10, 1958. Following the ceremony, a turkey dinner was served to 80 guests at the Community Hall. The Ramblers from Cardston was the orchestra for the dance. Refreshments were served. Members of the Homemakers Club and the Peigan W.A. assisted Mrs. Scott with the serving at dinner and dance.

A banquet and ball, honoring Senator Jim Gladstone, a member of the Blood Indian tribe, was held February 18, 1958, at the St. Paul's Indian Residential School, Cardston. Many people from the Peigan Reserve attended.

Mary Jane Born With A Tooth is a patient in the Charles Camsell Hospital in Edmonton. While she is away her daughter Joyce, Mrs. Tommy No Runner, is here from Browning to take care of the little ones at home.

Welcome Home to Guy Yellow Wings who has been a patient in the Camsell Hospital.

Sincere sympathy to the families in which there have been deaths: Mr. Wes Miller died Feb. 2; little Harold John Sharp Adze, Feb. 25; and Mrs. Nora North Peigan on March 5, 1958.

There are three new babies: Verna Polly Warrior, born December 1, 1957, daughter of Pete and Colette Warrior; Adrian Murray North Peigan, born Dec. 22, 1957, son of Hartwell and Mona North Peigan; and Sheldon Earl Crazy Boy, born February 2, 1958, son of Mick and Annie Crazy Boy.

The total of Little Helpers is now 106. The book with their names and birthdays is kept in St. Cyprian's Church, Brocket.

The Peigan W.A. had the election of officers in January. Josephine Crow Shoe is President; Gertie Bastien and Marion Crow Shoe are Vice-Presidents; Margaret Plain Eagle is Secretary; and Elsie Bray is Treasurer and Sewing Convener. Members are doing embroidery work, and have been busy with frequent Rummage Sales.

ST. CYPRIAN'S SCHOOL W.A. by Miss Mason, Secretary
as taken from The Anglican Newsletter dated Easter, 1958

The St. Cyprian's School W.A. meets every second Tuesday, with six members in attendance. One of our projects for the year is making up and distributing baby bundles. These are for all new-born Anglican babies on the reserve. We also have been making and selling costume jewelry. The World Day of Prayer Service was used at a regular meeting with all members participating. We are now working on the study of Japan.

EYE DOCTOR'S VISIT by Mildred Woodman, grade 5
as taken from the Anglican Newsletter, Easter, 1958

In December the eye doctor came to our school to check our eyes. He used our day-room, with blankets over the windows to make it dark. Then some girls and I went down to see him. He put something in our eyes, and told us to go back to class. After a while we went back. He told me I needed glasses. Finally, I was fixed up. A lot of children got glasses. These are the ones: Sharon Crow Shoe, Helen Weasel Bear, Delma Crow Shoe, Vera North Peigan, Hazel Weasel Bear, Eileen North Peigan, Butch Weasel Bear, and myself. Also some children in the junior classroom. Now we see lots better.

DENTIST'S VISIT by Vera North Peigan, grade 5

On February 27 the dentist payed a visit to this school. From the Senior Classroom there were three of us girls and no boys at all who had teeth fixed. I guess there were eight from the Junior Classroom. I had two teeth filled. It hurt a little when he drilled, but I soon got over it. The dentist said we all have good teeth.

DID YOU KNOW?

Joe Crow Shoe, Jr. is now a cadet with the Peigan Cadet Corps, but when he leaves school he says he wants to join the P.P.C.L.I. (Please Protect Canada's Little Indians!)

Arnold Crazy Boy's ambition is to be a lazy farmer.

A SMILE:

    Tom: "What did the little porcupine say when he backed up into a cactus?"
    Bill: "I don't know, Tom, what did he say?"
    Tom: He said, "Is that you, Mom?"

NOTES FROM THE GROUPS
as written in The Anglican Newsletter, Easter, 1958

G.A. News, by Miss E. Bray, leader

The G.A. girls are busy at their meetings each week. They are making leather purses for themselves; embroidering pillow cases, aprons, and pot holders; and they have started on a quilt. They hope to earn their Dorcas Badges.

J.A. News, by Sandra North Peigan, grade 4

This year we have elected regular officers for our J.A. The president is Hazel Weasel Bear. The secretary is Sandra North Peigan, and the treasurer is Patsy Yellow Horn.

Our badge work is progressing very well. One of our members has her Churchmanship Badge.

For our activity work we are learning how to make a quilt for our doll's bed. Sometimes one of the girls chooses a special activity, and then she has to figure out what things she will need to do it. At another meeting she shows the other girls how to do it.

We wish everyone a Happy Easter.

Junior Sewing Class

Sunday School, by Kenneth Yellow Horn, grade 4

We have Sunday School every Sunday at half past three. We go to the chapel first. We sing two hymns and we pray. After, we go to our classes, and we say our verses. Then we have our books and read what is in them. When we have finished our work, we go downstairs.

Singsong, by Sandra North Peigan, grade 4

Every second Sunday the grades 4 to 7 go to the chapel at 7:30 for a singsong. We sing from our hymn books or song sheets. Sometimes Mr. Stanger uses his recorder and lets us hear our singing. At our last singsong he asked us to say our names, and then he played them back to us. I like when we have our singsong.

Square Dance Club, by Betty Ann Crow Shoe, grade 7

We have our square dancing every Monday night. We go down to Brocket about eight o'clock. During Lent we are having games instead of dancing. We all like going. There are eleven members from here.

Manual Training, by George Weasel Bear, grade 7

as taken from The Anglican Newsletter, Easter, 1958

We grade 6 and 7 boys go to manual training class every Friday morning down in Brocket. The day school boys come too. Bob Thornton is our instructor. He teaches us how to use tools and how to make things. Some of us have made cabinets, benches, suitcases, and corner shelves. We make anything we want to make.

Junior Boys League, by Miss E. Bray

There are 12 boys in the J.B.L.
When we're together we sure can yell.
We meet with Evelyn, Wednesday at 4:
If you read on we'll tell you some more.
At handicrafts, we're not very good,
The things we make, some are of wood.
Paper and paste, scissors and paint,
Are freely used to make objects quaint.
Our penny collection is getting large,
One for each meeting, as we are charged.
Hope you'll like our autographs,
The little drawings are to make you laugh.

Church Boys League, by John Stanger, grade 3

as printed in The Anglican Newsletter, Easter, 1958

We stand to form a cross for the opening of our meeting. The shield-bearer holds the shield. The scribe calls the roll, and the boys answer saying the motto. The keeper-of-the-purse takes our pennies and says the pledge prayer. Sir Joe leads the opening service.

Lots of boys are soon going to have their sandals-of-peace badge.

Sometimes we play games, and sometimes we have stories. We've made leather belts, flower pots, painted chairs and sleds, and coloured pictures.

We made a scrapbook for the Peigan Hospital.

Soon we are going to learn lots of things about Japan.

Our Friar visited our meeting one day. He helped us learn more about our pledge-of-loyalty, and before he left we had a sing-song.

One day we could not have a real meeting. The piano-tuner was using the room to fix the piano. We all went to the boys' playroom and played games with the J.B.L. boys.

We like to have C.B.L. every Wednesday.

HEALTH IN WORK AND PLAY

NOTES FROM THE GROUPS

as taken from The Anglican Newsletter, June, 1958

Senior W.A. by L.K. How

The St. Cyprian's Senior W.A. held the closing meeting of this school term on June 7. We have completed our study on Japan, and have finished our projects. Our closing meeting took the form of a dinner party, which was held in the Stanger's apartment. After dinner, we enjoyed a social evening listening to records and tape recordings. We are looking forward to starting our meetings again in the fall.

G.A., by E. Bray, leader

The seven members of St. Cyprian's G.A. and their leader attended the G.A. Rally in Calgary on May 10. The girls had finished their quilt with embroidered Indian scenes, and had coloured a map of Japan to display there. After a very enjoyable day at Paget Hall with 150 other girls, a trip to St. George's Island was enjoyed by all. Rev. Stanger drove the group to Calgary, and while there we all had a very nice visit with Miss Higgins.

At the last meeting of the G.A. group, Betty Ann Crow Shoe was presented with a gift. She was the highest on the average for work done during the term.

Sunday School

On June 22, 1958, at the regular classes, the Sunday school teachers made awards for general proficiency, as follows:

Miss Bayne's beginners - first, Linda Yellow Horn
    second, Eric North Peigan and Douglas Yellow Horn
Miss Crow Shoe's level 2 - first, Ruby Crow Shoe
Miss How's level 3 - first, Mary Born With A Tooth
Mrs. Ellis's level 4 - first, Patsy Yellow Horn
    second, Kenneth Yellow Horn

Miss Mason's levels 5 & 6 - first, Judy Stanger
    second, Sammy Born With A Tooth
    third, Woodrow North Peigan
    fourth, Mildred Woodman and Hazel Weasel Bear
Miss Bray's level 7 - first, Joe Crow Shoe
    second, Agnes Strikes With A Gun
    third, Arnold Crazy Boy and George Weasel Bear

WHIRLAWAY DANCE CLUB, by Evelyn Crow Shoe, secretary-treasurer as take from The Anglican Newsletter, June, 1958

The square dance season has ended again and I would like to take this opportunity to thank all who turned out. Everyone did very well in learning some difficult dances, as well as the easy ones.

Up until Christmas, Mr. Opperman, Mr. Beatton and others from Pincher Creek came out to help us. On behalf of the club, thanks to those folks for helping us, and for the use of the records, phonograph and amplifier. Next term we hope to have more equipment, more adult members coming out regularly, and some new members too.

Have a nice summer all of you, and thanks a million.

SEWING CLASSES
as taken from The Anglican Newsletter, June, 1958

Junior Class: We six girls met Tuesdays from 4:15 to 5:15. At first we practiced hemming on the sewing machine. Then we made baby dresses.

Mildred, Hazel and Judy made aprons. Delma, Sandra and Patsy made nightgowns. We all made half-slips, skirts and blouses.

We tried a few simple stitches in embroidery and crochet.

We enjoyed our sewing lessons, and hope we can have a sewing class next term.

Senior Class: We seven girls met on Thursday evenings. We made slips and cotton gingham dresses. Some of the girls made denim skirts. Everything turned out very nice.

HANDICRAFTS, by E. Bray, leader
as taken from The Anglican Newsletter, June, 1958

Handicraft classes are over for this term. The boys made belts, bookends, and laced purses and wallets.

The girls did purses, beaded change purses, beaded necklaces and bracelets, and a lot of embroidery work on pillow cases and aprons. A number of these things are being entered in the Calgary and Edmonton Exhibitions. Others are for sale or for the boys and girls to take home with them.

SPORTS
as taken from The Anglican Newsletter, June, 1958

Since spring, the main sport has been softball. Games were played by the boys against High Bush, and against the Sacred Heart School. The girls played against the Sacred Heart girls, too. The scores ??? (we can't tell!).

We have had some volleyball too. The girls think they are ready to beat the boys, but we need some dry weather to prove this.

THE CHURCH BOYS' LEAGUE, by L. Stanger, leader

The C.B.L. is an official organization of the Anglican Church of Canada. First formed in 1930, it was completely re-organized in 1956. The present C.B.L. is based on the twelfth century Knighthood.

A member joins the league as a Page. He must pass certain requirements to become an Esquire, and he reaches the culmination of his training when he becomes a Knight, dedicated to serve the King of Kings (Jesus Christ.) During this process he wins, in the form of crests, his whole armour: the girdle of truth, the breastplate of righteousness, the sandals of peace, the shield of faith, the helmet of salvation, and the sword of the spirit. (Ephesians 6: 13-17)

Older boys - up to 20 years of age - may become Knight Counsellors of the Cross, and Knights of the Round Table.

St. Cyprian's C.B.L. (new style) was first formed in September, 1957. We have 18 members in three bands, and we meet after school on Wednesdays. The boys have the uniform shirts, ties, and belts. We have made a shield for use at our meetings. For our opening and closing services everyone stands together so as to form a cross.

Meeting have been held on Wednesdays after school. This school term the boys have made checker blocks, spool toys, plaques, doll cribs, flower pots, leather belts, pictures, scrapbook, wire and string horses and cowboys. They have learned new games, and enjoyed the story of Kenji. We've gone on a few route marches - and nearly every boy knows his left foot from his right foot now! We have had two parties and some singsongs. At Christmas, the boys painted sleds for the little children. In February, we joined with the other church groups at the school in the World Day Of Prayer service.

Each boy is now an Esquire. Several have the Shield of Faith, and everyone hopes to have the complete armour next term.

JUNIOR BOYS' LEAGUE, by Evelyn Crow Shoe, leader, as taken from The Anglican Newsletter, June, 1958

The Junior Boys League had their last meeting for this term June 18. They have met every Wednesday from 4:15 - 5:15. They have had a good time making puppets, tepees, painting, drawing, doing cutouts, playing games, singing, and having P.T. They also made little drawers from match boxes thanks to a donation of boxes from Mrs. Jackie Crow Shoe. The little boys' favorite song was -

>Row, row, row your boat,
>Underneath the stream.
>Ha, ha, fooled you -
>I'm a submarine!

THE SUNBEAMS, by E. Bayne, leader
as taken from The Anglican Newsletter, June, 1958

The seven little sunbeams had their last meeting, for this term, May 28. Linda, Valerie, and Melinda each received a prize for good work and good conduct at meetings.

We tried to have variety at meetings. We colored pictures and made our own Mother Goose Book. At Christmas each girl made a picture for her mother - as well as a small gift for Mother's Day. At Easter they made Easter baskets. Each meeting we had a play period and a Bible story.

The girls have enjoyed having a group of their own, and look forward to a better year in the 1958-59 term.

LOCAL NEWS, by E. Bray, as submitted to The Anglican Newsletter, June, 1958

Mrs. Eileen Grier is a patient in the Col. Belcher Hospital in Calgary.

Jim Morning Bull is recovering from 'flu. He has been a patient in St. Vincent's Hospital for three weeks.

Confirmation was held in St. Cyprian's Church, Brocket, April 20. Those confirmed were George Weasel Bear, Arnold Crazy Boy, Woodrow North Peigan, Sharon Crow Shoe, Eileen North Peigan, Betty Ann Crow Shoe, and Agnes Strikes With A Gun - all from the residential school. Also confirmed were Wallace Yellow Face, Alan Red Young Man, Stewart Prairie Chicken, Maude Potts, and Evalina Iron Shirt - all from the reserve. After the service a reception was held in the community hall. Lunch was served by members of the Peigan W.A.

Mick and Annie Crazy Boy, Roy and Beatrice Big Bull, and Mary Sharp Adze have gone to pick strawberries at Sedro Wooley, in Washington.

Ethel and Ben Buffalo went berry picking at Creston, B.C.

Mary Jane Born With A Tooth is now home from the Charles Camsell.

Herbert White Owl had an accident on the highway, and is now a patient in the Charles Camsell Hospital in Edmonton.

Marion Crow Shoe is now on the staff at St. Cyprian's School.

The wedding of Donat Shining Double and Violet North Peigan took place at St. Cyprian's Church, Brocket, April 12, 1958. The Rev. Doyle of Fort Macleod officiated.

The new babies are: Gayleen Marie, daughter of Yvonne North Peigan; Karen Anne, daughter of Anne Mary and Edward Crow Shoe; Gailard Earl, son of Mary and Teddy Meat Face; Alvin Dean, son of Dorothy and Eddy Yellow Horn; Carol Faye, daughter of Jessie Crow Shoe; and Ophelia Blossom Joy, daughter of Lily and Richard Crow Shoe.

Little Helpers: There are 112 names on the Roll Call now. Plans are made for a party to be held early in the fall instead of at Christmas.

Peigan W.A: The W.A. have had a successful year, and are closing for the summer. They hope to have a picnic by Castle River before starting in September.

RIDDLES:

(1) What starts with a T, ends with a T, and is full of T?

(2) What is the strongest day of the week?

(3) When is a baseball player like a spider?

(4) Why are fish so educated?

Answers: 1) a teapot 2) Sunday; all the rest are weekdays (weak) days.   3) When he catches flies.   4) They live in schools.

A TYPICAL DAY AT ST. CYPRIAN'S I.R.S.
by three girls from the senior classroom: Mildred, Judy and Agnes, as found in the The Anglican Newsletter, June, 1958

We get up at 6:30 in the morning, get our clothes on, make our beds, and tidy up our dorm. Then we go downstairs and wash our faces and comb out hair. We get our aprons on ready for breakfast.

At ten after seven four girls go into the dining room to serve the food out. Two girls put the food out, and two girls the drink. We all get into line waiting for the breakfast bell to ring. When it rings we go to our places, say our grace, and eat. After, some girls wash the dishes, sweep the floor, and wash the tables.

Other boys and girls have their chores to do. Those that are not on the work lists may go outside to play. When it is near nine o'clock we all get ready to go to the chapel to worship God. We sing a hymn, have a story, say prayers. When the minister says the closing prayer we come out of the chapel and go to our classrooms.

Recess is at 10:30. We get out for noon at 12:00. We have our dinner at 12:15. After dinner some of the girls go in to wash dishes, and help clean up the dining room and kitchen. Others go out to play. We get washed. 1:30 is the time for all to go back to classes. Recess is at a quarter to three. Classes are over for the day at four o'clock.

At 4:15 activities go on. Certain days we have group meetings, sports, handicrafts, walks, work, or T.V. Juniors get their teeth brushed, and all ready for bed by 7:30. Seniors by 8:30.

When we are ready for bed, we kneel down beside our beds and say our prayers together. Then we get into bed to have a long, happy night's sleep, and be ready for the next busy day.

THE GRADUATES OF ST. CYPRIAN'S SCHOOL
as found in The Anglican Newsletter, June, 1958

Joe Crow Shoe is the senior boy at St. Cyprian's, and the one and only Army Cadet. He is a C.B.L. member, and has proven himself a good sport in softball and hockey. Joe's hobbies are leathercraft and art. Also, he has turned out quite nice woodwork at Manual Training.

Joe hopes to take a course in mechanics and we hope that he will make it. His favorite expression is "Get Lost!" Joe has been Miss Bray's "right hand man" all year. He'll be greatly missed by all. Best of luck, Joe.

Eileen North Peigan is a great rock 'n roll fan, and is usually heard singing an Elvis Presley song. Her favorite song just now is "The Story Of My Life." We are going to miss her singing, and also her playing the mouth organ. Eileen has earned three badges in Girls' Auxiliary and has been doing some bead work.

Her ambition was to be a lady wrestler - we wonder if it still is! We also wonder who is going to be Agnes' jiving partner now that Eileen is going? And who will be the girls' best softball pitcher? Best of everything from us all, Eileen.

Sharon Crow Shoe is constantly seen with her nose in a book. She enjoys singing, writing letters, and has done a lot of beadwork this year. Sharon has been a member of the Girls' Auxiliary, and has earned three badges.

Sharon's favorite song is "All I Do Is Dream." And her favorite expression is, "I don't care."

All the best, Sharon.

Helen Weasel Bear, so the class says, makes lovely pies! She has proven a great help in the dining room. While in G.A., Helen has earned eight badges, and this year held the office of president.

Helen's hobbies are reading and beadwork. She also enjoys singing, cooking, and dancing. We wish you, Helen, the best of everything in whatever you may do.

· · · NEWS FLASH · · ·

June, 1958, academic awards:

Miss How, junior classroom teacher, reports the following pupils are the first prize winners:

    Grade 1 A - Linda Yellow Horn

    Grade 1 B - Vernon Morning Bull

    Grade 2 A - Billy North Peigan

    Grade 2 B - Linda North Peigan and Glennis Crow Shoe

    Grade 3 - Gerald Crazy Boy

And a special prize, for general improvement, goes to Woodrow Crow Eagle, grade two.

Miss Mason, senior classroom teacher, reports the following top students:

    Grade 4 - Patsy Yellow Horn, with 82%

    Grade 5 - Mildred Woodman, with 95.2%

    Grade 6 - Woodrow North Peigan, with 72%

    Grade 7 - Betty Ann Crow Shoe, with 67.8%

· · · CONGRATULATIONS · · ·

School's Out!

School is closing, hurray, hurray!
We're looking forward to our holiday.
We'll swim, pick berries and get a good tan,
And try to keep our clothes spic and span.

This term has gone by so very quick -
We hope our vacation won't do the same trick!
One thing we know - when September begins,
We'll all be back with big wide grins.

We'll take care of ourselves
Whatever we do.
Goodbye! Good Luck!
From us to you.

IN THE GOOD OLD SUMMERTIME:

CHAPTER SIX

SCHOOL TERM: 1958 - 1959

ST. CYPRIAN'S RESIDENTIAL SCHOOL STAFF, to begin the 1958-59 school year:

Rev. Stanger, Principal

Mrs. Stanger, Matron

> WEDDING BELLS: 1958
> Early in September, Mrs. Ellis and Mr. Doolittle were married quietly.
> Mr. and Mrs. Doolittle continue their work here at St. Cyprian's

Mrs. Fidler, Cook

Miss Bayne, Seamstress

Miss How, Junior Teacher

.... Senior Teacher

Mrs. Doolittle, Girls' Supervisor

Miss Bray, Boys' Supervisor

Miss Crow Shoe, General Assistant and Recreational Supervisor

Mr. Doolittle and Mr. Brown, Maintenance

TRAINEES: (*girls recently graduated from this school who have returned to work here*)

Miss Helen Weasel Bear, Cook's Helper

Miss Helen Strikes With A Gun, Laundress

Miss Evelyn Crazy Boy, General Helper

PUPILS:

Junior Classroom - 38 boys and girls (Miss How, teacher)

    Beginners: 5
    Grade One: 9
    Grade Two: 7
    Grade Three: 17

Senior classroom - 23 boys and girls (no teacher, as yet)

    Grade Four   7
    Grade Five   5
    Grade Six   6
    Grade Seven 1
    Grade Eight 4

Note: Joe Crow Shoe and Sharon Crow Shoe, graduates last term, have chosen to come back for further education.

THANKSGIVING, 1958
excerpts taken from The Anglican Newsletter, as submitted by Rev. Stanger

Greetings, and Happy Thanksgiving to all friends of *St. Cyprian's* and to all readers of *The Anglican Newsletter.*

We have begun our 1958-59 school term, and we hope that this year's voyage on the *sea of education* will be a voyage not fraught with more storms than our vessel and crew can manage. However, at the time of *going to press* we are minus one teacher. Somewhere along the line we were missed, and a teacher was not supplied to replace Miss Mason who has gone to Frog Lake, Alberta. While our good wishes are with Miss Mason, we wonder ... *Oh where, oh where, can our teacher be?* Thus far, we have been fortunate in having substitute teachers for the senior classroom thanks to Mr. L. Legge, and Mrs. Ivens. Miss How, as usual, has her junior classroom work well under way.

At this Thanksgiving season let us be thankful for the bounty of the harvest, the blessings of friends, family, good health. and shelter from the winds that rattle the windows. May our thanksgivings also strengthen our trust and faith in the future, and keep us mindful that some of the things we are denied may indeed be gifts as well.

Blind Ploughman
by Radclyffe Hall

Set my hands upon the plough,
My feet upon the sod;
Turn my face towards the east,
And praise be to God!

Every year the rains do fall,
The seeds they stir and spring;
Every year the spreading trees,
Shelter birds that sing.

From the shelter of your heart,
Brother - drive out sin,
Let the little birds of faith
Come and nest therein.

God has made His sun to shine
On both you and me;
God, who took away my eyes,
That my soul might see!

LOCAL NEWS, by E. Bray
as submitted to The Anglican Newsletter, Thanksgiving, 1958

The Indian Days Festival was held in Brocket on August 28 and 29. Due to cloudy and windy weather many of the activities were cancelled.

The Rev. and Mrs. Cuthand and family were visitors to St. Cyprian's in August, and Rev. Cuthand took services at St. Cyprian's Church in Brocket.

Another August visitor to the school was Mrs. Mills, from Shediac, N.B. She is in the W.A. down east, and was very interested in our school and activities.

Jim Morning Bull is a patient in the Charles Camsell Hospital, Edmonton.

Mervyn Crow Shoe, George Crow Shoe, Lewis Strikes With A Gun, Roderick North Peigan, and Betty Ann Crow Shoe are going to school in Pincher Creek. Wayne Knowlton is taking his grade nine by correspondence at Brocket Day School.

In July, Joe Crow Shoe, Sr. attended the Layman's Conference at Watrous Beach for two weeks.

Evelyn and Mervyn Crow Shoe took the Recreational Leader's Training Course at Red Deer in July. They are now using their knowledge and skill on the reserve. One of their enterprises is the Brocket Whirlaway Square Dance Club which started on September 15, with good attendance each week.

Leslie Plain Eagle had an operation for mastoids recently.

Frances Rabbit was a recent visitor in Brocket.

Welcome to Brocket: Mr. and Mrs. Tony Duckett and sons, and Mr. and Mrs. Hoskins.

The new babies on the reserve are all girls, daughters to Alice and Matthew One Owl, Betty Ann Crow Shoe, Beatrice and Roy Big Bull, and Elsie Crow Shoe.

Mr. Leonard Legge substituted in the senior classroom at St. Cyprian's for a week, until he had to leave for the University of Edmonton.

A farewell party was held at the Woodsworth's home for Miss Richter who left the Nursing Station to take a course in welfare work.

The Peigan W.A. are making plans for Thanksgiving, and for the Little Helpers' annual party. President Josephine Crow Shoe hopes that all members will make an effort to attend each meeting this term.

Junior News

In our room we have three bears, Father Bear, Mother Bear and Baby Bear.

We saw a big moose go past the school. It was black.

We have a new globe. It is big.

We have a Bible story every day. We heard about Adam and Eve, Cain and Abel, Jacob and Esau, and Joseph.

We have P.T. with Miss Crow Shoe every week.

One day the boys met a skunk. Poor boys!!

We have five new pupils —
Bryan Yellow Horn
Jeffrey Crow Shoe
Philip Big Swan
Betty Crazy Boy
Howard One Owl.

SMILES:

Hula Hoop, Hula Hoop,
One for each in the group
Sam and Jerry - Mel and Bill
Walking 'round or standing still.

They wiggle their hips and twist around,
The Hula Hoop circles up and down.
It's great for exercise or for fun,
Soon everybody will have one.

. . .

- One little girl says, *"Gee, Mr. Doolitle sure runs fast with his car!"*

- But then, our Mr. Doolittle says things like this:

    Strawberries are my favourite vegetable.
    If I ever tell the truth, I'll sure apologize.
    When my holidays come, I'll have to stop pretending to work.
    I'm certainly not two-faced, or else I'd use the other one.
    It's OK if you charge it, long as you don't try to collect.
    I know you're honest, but then I'm an awful liar.

SOME OF OUR ACTIVITIES
as taken from The Anglican Newsletter, Thanksgiving, 1958

Our Dining Room, by Caroline Yellow Horn, *grade 4*

We have new curtains in our dining room. We sit in different places this year. The cutlery girls have new basins this year. Thirty-two boys and thirty-one girls eat in the children's dining room.

The Square Dance Club, by Mildred Woodman, *grade 6*

We go down to the hall every Monday night to do some dancing. Mr. Stanger takes us down at twenty minutes to eight. We go in the truck. The pupils that are in the Square Dance Club are Sharon Crow Shoe, Mildred Woodman, Hazel Weasel Bear, Annabelle Buffalo, Patsy Yellow Horn, Sandra North Peigan, Joe Crow Shoe, Butch Weasel Bear, Arnold Crazy Boy, Woodrow North Peigan, Sammy Born With A Tooth, Ronnie Morning Bull, Clifford Crow Shoe and Walter Crow Shoe.

The staff that go are Miss Bray, Miss Crow Shoe. The trainees go too. They are Helen Weasel Bear, Evelyn Crazy Boy, and Helen Strikes With A Gun. We have very much fun dancing. At about ten o'clock Mr. Stanger comes to the hall to take us back to school. I will say again we have very much fun in dancing club.

Our Physical Training, by Patsy Yellow Horn, *grade 5*

We, the senior girls, have our P.T. on Wednesday, and the Junior Girls on Thursday afternoon. Miss Crow Shoe teaches us. It is fun.

Junior Auxiliary, by Betty Red Young Man, *grade 4*

On Sunday we have our J.A. at 2:30. All the groups go to the chapel for a service together. Then we go to our own groups. There we have badge work or activity. We also have games and sometimes a story. Judy Stanger is helping our leader this year. Caroline is the president, and Betty the secretary.

Handicrafts, by Sharon Crow Shoe, *grade 8*

We have our handicrafts on Friday nights, from 6:30 to 8:30. The girls with Miss Crow Shoe, and the boys with Miss Bray. We meet in the boys' playroom. Annabelle, Mildred, Judy, and Hazel are making slippers. I am making a belt. In our handicraft class we have the boys and girls from grades five, six, seven, and eight. We sure have a lot of fun making things.

Our G.A. by Helen Weasel Bear, *grade 8*

There are six members in our G.A. We held an election of officers to start our new term. Mildred Woodman is president, Hazel Weasel Bear is vice-president, Sharon Crow Shoe is secretary-treasurer. Our leader is Miss Bray. We meet every week. Handicrafts of all kinds will be done this term. We shall all work at a quilt, then do beadwork, leather work, embroidery, felt work, and we are going to try copper tooling. I know we are going to have a successful year and you'll hear from us again.

The St. Cyprian's Senior W.A. had the opening meeting of the term on October 6, 1958. Devotional, educational, and social service programs were drawn up as a guide to the year's work.

The Sunbeams are six little girls meeting with Miss Bayne, as last year.

The JBL has fifteen little boys meeting under the leadership of Miss Crow Shoe, while her brother, Joe, the senior boy here, is her assistant.

The CBL the older boys' group, are meeting again regularly with Mrs. Stanger. She chose as her helpers George Weasel Bear and Arnold Crazy Boy. The scribe is Clifford Crow Shoe, and the keeper-of-the-purse is Woodrow North Peigan.

WELL, DID YOU EVER! *by Miss How and Miss Bray*

Did you ever see?

- a WHITE COW on a horse
- a little BIG BULL
- a pretty PLAIN EAGLE
- a CRAZY BOY girl
- a MORNING BULL at night
- a STRIKES WITH A GUN playing baseball
- a GOOD RIDER walking
- a YELLOW FACE blushing
- a BIG SMOKE with no fire
- a WOOD MAN cooking with gas

WHAT KIND ARE YOU?

A lot of Christians are like wheelbarrows - no good unless pushed.
Some are like canoes - they need to be paddled.
Some are like kites - if you don't keep a string on them they fly away.
Some are like kittens - they are more content when petted.
Some are like balloons - full of air and ready to blow up.
Some are like trailers - they have to be pulled.
Some are like neon lights - they keep going on and off.
Some are like a good watch: open face, pure gold, quietly busy, and full of good works.

A CHRISTMAS POEM,
by Miss How
as taken from The Anglican Newsletter,
Christmas edition, 1958

He was only a little donkey
So quiet and shaggy and brown,
But he carried the mother of Jesus
As they went to Bethlehem town.
It was just a rough little stable
Behind a crowded inn,
But it housed the little Messiah
Who would save the world from sin.
He was such a little baby
As on Mary's lap he lay,
But he would grow to manhood
To be Prince of Peace one day.
God still uses the little things
To show his love today,
A word of praise, a friendly smile,
A lift along the way.
And these make for a merry Christmas,
And a happy New Year too,
But what is more, they make Christmas
Last the whole year through.

SANTA CLAUS AND THE MOUSE
a recitation by Mary Born With A Tooth, grade 4
as presented at the Christmas Concert, 1958

On Christmas Eve, when Santa Claus
Came to a certain house,
To fill the children's stockings there,
He found a little mouse.
"A merry Christmas, little friend,"
Said Santa, good and kind.
"The same to you, sir," said the mouse;
"I thought you wouldn't mind...
"If I should stay awake tonight
And watch you for a while."
"You're very welcome, little mouse,"
Said Santa, with a smile.
And then he filled the stockings up
Before the mouse could wink -
From toe to top, from top to toe,
There wasn't left a chink.
"Now, they won't hold another thing,"
Said Santa Claus, with pride.
A twinkle came in mouse's eyes,
But humbly he replied:
"It's not polite to contradict-
Your pardon I implore-
But in the fullest stocking there
I could put one thing more."
"Oh, ho!" laughed Santa, "silly mouse,
Don't I know how to pack?
By filling stockings all these years,

I should have learned the knack."
And then he took the stocking down
From where it hung so high,
And said, "Now put in one thing more;
I give you leave to try."
The mousie chuckled to himself,
And then he softly stole
Right to the stocking's crowded toe,
And gnawed a little hole!
"Now, if you please, good Santa Claus,
I've put in one thing more;
For you will know that little hole
Was not in there before."
How Santa Claus did laugh and laugh!
And then he gaily spoke:
"Well you shall have a Christmas cheese
For that nice little joke."
If you don't think this story true,
Why! I can show to you
The very stocking with the hole
The little mouse gnawed through.

Junior Auxiliary
as taken from The Anglican Newsletter, Christmas, 1958

A skit, "No Trains Today."
as presented at the Christmas Concert

The Scene is a railway crossing:

Abner and Alvina, a backwoods couple, approach the crossing, and look cautiously *up* the track. Abner then goes to the stationmaster and ascertains that there aren't any trains going *east* today.

He reports this information to his dear wife, and then they look *down* the track. Abner returns to the stationmaster and gets his word that there aren't any trains going *west* today -- that there just aren't any trains going anywhere today.

Abner rejoins his wife at the tracks and says, "Wahl, come on Alvina. It's safe t'cross them there tracks."

Judy Stanger played Alvina, Ruby Crow Shoe, the stationmaster, and the part of Abner was played by Mary Born With A Tooth.

The Church Boys' League
as presented at the Christmas Concert

A skit, "The Operation."

The Scene: Jimmy lying on an operating table. He has a severe stomach ache, and the doctor is proceeding to operate.

Then one by one the doctor removes all the things Jimmy ate at the picnic, and also his intestines, a few ribs, and his heart.

Then he sews him up and says, "Too bad. He was such a nice boy. Call the undertaker."

At that very moment, heart or no heart, Jimmy jumps up shrieking - and races out!

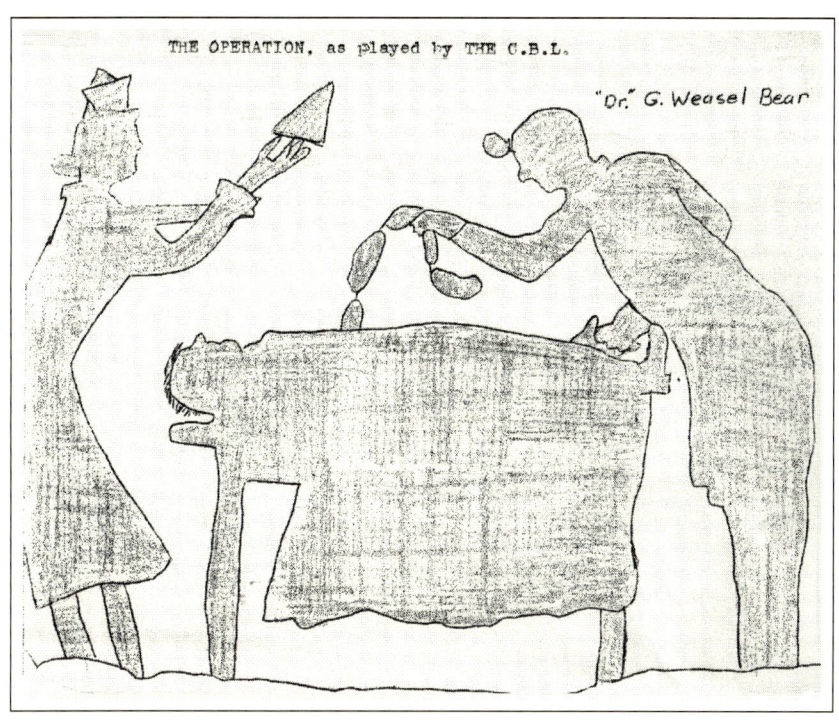

SMILES:

Junior: "What do you repair shoes with?"
Shoemaker: "Hide."
Junior: "What?"
Shoemaker: "Hide. Hide! The cow's outside."
Junior: "I don't care if it is. I'm not afraid of a cow."

• • •

Son: "Dad, that liniment really makes my arm smart."
Dad: "That's good. Try rubbing some of it on your head, too."

LOCAL NEWS, by E. Bray
as printed in The Anglican Newsletter, December, 1958

Frances Smith was married, Dec. 4 to Ralph Weasel Fat at St. Paul's School, Cardston. They will make their home in Cardston.

A successful *Indoor Track and Field Meet* was held by some members of the Whirlaway Dance Club, in November.

Little Miss Marilyn Crow Shoe returned home after a long visit with her grandparents, Chief and Mrs. McHugh of Gleichen.

New babies: a boy, John Stanger Bull Pen, to Ida and Tom Bull Pen; a girl, Sharon, to Bridget and Earnest North Peigan; a boy, Frederick Lee, to Julianna and Freddy North Peigan; a boy, Alphonse Richard, to Margaret and Jim Plain Eagle.

New patients in Charles Camsell Hospital are Vincent Big Bull and infant Frederick Lee North Peigan. Mrs. O'Keefe is a patient in St. Vincent's Hospital, Pincher Creek. And Sam Provost is ill at home.

George Crow Shoe and Peter Yellow Horn are playing basketball for the High School in Pincher Creek.

The Peigan W.A. met at Josephine Crow Shoe's for their annual Christmas party, Thursday Dec. 11. During the past few months, meetings were held in the Hall. Several rummage sales were held to raise money. The ladies would like to take this opportunity of saying *Thank You* to everyone who has generously donated to the group. A blessed Christmas to all.

The Little Helpers annual party was held as planned on Dec. 9. There were 76 little ones there with parents. A short service was held by Rev. Doyle. Games were played under the supervision of Miss Evelyn Crow Shoe. Lunch was served by Josephine and Evelyn Crow Shoe, Margaret Plain Eagle, Miss Bray, and Rev.

Doyle. Gifts were given to all the youngsters before the enjoyable afternoon came to a close.

A cantata, *Little Red Riding Hood*, is being presented by the choir of Christ Church, Fort Macleod, in the community hall on Friday, Dec. 12. The proceeds are for the Peigan W.A.

SMILE:

"Hey, where are you going? Your pudding is just starting to boil."

"Yes, I know, but the recipe said *as soon as it begins to boil, beat it.*"

FROM THE EDITOR: L. M. Stanger,
as taken from The Anglican Newsletter, Christmas, 1958

I want to take this opportunity to thank each and every one of our readers, and especially those of you who wrote to us during the year with encouragement.

Preparing *The Newsletter* really is a lot of fun. It is also a big job now that our circulation is well over three hundred. To have your comments is a big help; the favorable ones keep us going full steam ahead, and your suggestions and requests give us new vision.

To one and to all, and on behalf of all who make *The Anglican Newsletter* possible, I wish you a very Merry Christmas, and a truly Happy New Year.

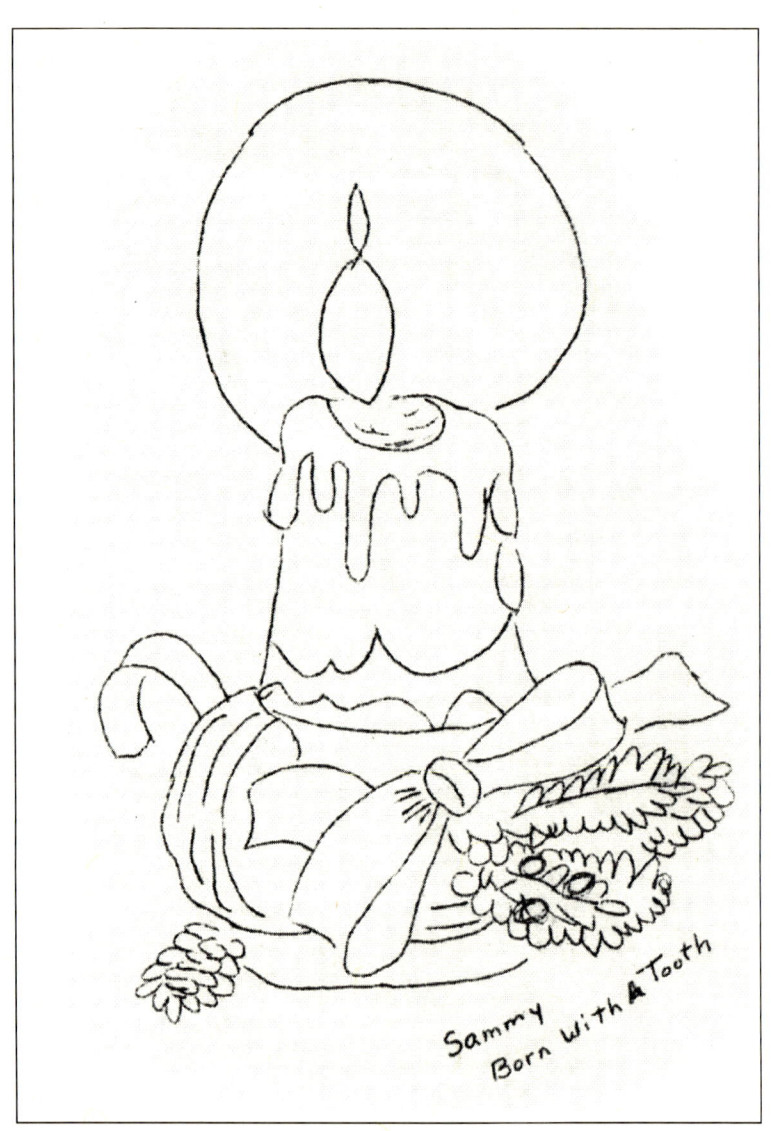

WHAT SHALL I DO WITH MY LIFE? by L.M. Stanger, newsletter editor.

Martha Constant, from Fort a la Corne, knows what she wants to do with her life. During her last year in high school she decided she wanted to qualify as a teacher - to teach in day schools on a reserve amongst her own people. Now, with help and encouragement in the right direction, Martha is attending Teachers' College, Saskatoon.

Two young men from the John Smith Reservation:

- Joe Louis Bear was a grade twelve graduate in 1958. In grade eleven he had top marks in physics, and in grade twelve received a character award. Also, he received one of the fifteen scholarship awards given in Canada. He is now taking X-Ray Technology training in Regina.

- The Reverend Daniel Umperville was graduated from Wycliffe in 1953, and from Saskatoon Teachers' College in 1954. He was ordained a priest in 1957, and now serves as missionary and teacher on the Thunderchild Reservation.

From Red Pheasant Reservation:

- Ruby Soonias was graduated from Prince Albert Collegiate in 1957. She is training to be a nurse at Prince Albert's Victoria Hospital.

From Sandy Lake Reservation:

- Hazel Ahenekew was graduated from Prince Albert Collegiate in 1956. She works as a stenographer at the Indian Office, Lac La Ronge.

- Lester Isbister received the 1956 Tom Longboat medal. He is now on staff at Gordon's Indian Residential School.

From Mistawasis Reservation:

- Kate Pechawais is in second year nursing at Dauphin, Manitoba.

From Onion Lake:

- Percy Bird was a graduate of Prince Albert Collegiate in 1952. He is now in his final year at Emmanuel, and a holder of a Private Pilot's License. He is married with three children.

From La Pas, Manitoba;

- Wilma Whitehead was a graduate of the Prince Albert Collegiate in 1955. She became a Registered Nurse in February, 1958.

- Doris and Esther Young, twins, graduated from Prince Albert Collegiate in 1958. Doris is attending Saskatoon Business College, and Esther is taking nurse's training in Winnipeg.

- Stanley Wilson is in grade twelve at Prince Albert Collegiate. He plans to take his Bachelor of Education at the University of Saskatchewan. He won an Air Cadet Scholarship Award in 1957. He has his Private Pilot's License, and is holder of the 1958 Longboat Medal.

The initiative shown by those young people will prompt other First Nation pupils to say, *"I will do something worthwhile with my life."*

THIS AND THAT, by pupils of St. Cyprian's
as printed in the The Anglican Newsletter, Easter, 1959

Tra-la-tra-la:

The New Year brought good luck to St. Cyprian's; we got a teacher for the senior classroom. *Mrs. McGuffie*, born and raised in South Africa, recently came to Canada from England. (We will have the story of her life to share with you soon.)

Epidemic:

The Thing visited St. Cyprian's for the first two weeks of February. It found many friends here - forty-five in fact. These were mostly from the junior classroom. Most of the children were in bed, then out of bed, then in bed again. However, nearly all were back in classes by the end of the second week, and we hope *The Thing* has left us for good.

. . .

Poem
by George Weasel Bear

Half the class are sick in bed
Coughing their lungs to bits.
We give them supper and get them fed,
While the staff are having fits!

. . .

Copy Cats!

The senior boys are all trying to have their hair cut like Mr. Stanger's. The very willing barber is our senior boy of St. Cyprian's, Joe Crow Shoe.

Woodrow, the Winner:

The Easter newsletter's front cover is the result of a contest. Fourteen drawings were submitted by the pupils for this edition. The winning one[3] was done by Woodrow Crow Eagle, grade three.

World Day Of Prayer:

The first Friday in Lent, February 13, a World Day of Prayer Service was held in the school chapel at St. Cyprian's. Including all the groups, about 65 people attended. The service was built around the filmstrip entitled *The Voice of Prayer is Never Silent*. Missionary hymns were sung and prayers said for God's people all over the world.

JA Has A Pen Pal:

The Junior Auxiliary of St. Cyprian's now has a pen-pal. She is Joyce King-Hunter of Sunnybrook, Alberta. Joyce is a member of the newly formed Junior Partners.

Junior Partners was begun in consideration of girls who are remotely situated, and who take Sunday School by Post. These girls have no opportunity to belong to J.A. but can have some connection with the J.A. through this new organization. It also is an opportunity for J.A. groups to do some social service work.

Mrs. Doolittle, our J.A. leader, reports that we have sent money to help this new venture along.

---

[3] *See page 123 for the picture.*

The GA Knit And Cook:

The Girls' Auxiliary meeting of February 18 opened with a short service in the chapel led by the president, Mildred Crow Shoe. Then all members went to the staff sitting room for the remainder of the meeting. Minutes of the last meeting were read by the secretary, Sharon Crow Shoe. The adoption of the minutes was moved by Hazel Weasel Bear and seconded by Patsy Yellow Horn.

All members began knitting ankle socks. Plans were made for the girls to do baking on Monday nights to help them earn Cooking Badges. Some of the girls are also working on their Handicraft Badges. Before the meeting ended Mildred passed around cookies.

The following Monday, after cookies were baked - and eaten by the senior boys - we felt sure we had passed the test because this is what we heard:

Joe: They'll make good wives! (the girls he means)
George: Very good cooks!
Arnold: Taste like more.
Woodrow: Luscious!
Ronald: Thanks a lot. We'll come back for more.
Sam: Very good indeed!
Walter: Should do this every week. Thanks.
Ken: The more you eat the more you want.
Clifford: Makes my mouth water for more.

A SMILE:

Son: "Pop, are you growing taller all the time?"
Father: "No my son, why do you ask?"
Son: "Because the top of your head is poking up through your hair."

LOCAL NEWS, by E. Bray
as printed in The Anglican Newsletter, Easter, 1959

The annual meeting of the Peigan W.A. was held on January 9 in the community hall. Elected officers: Mrs. Joe Crow Shoe, president; vice-presidents, Gertie Bastien & Nellie Potts; secretary, Evelyn Crow Shoe; Treasurer and Little Helpers' secretary, Elsie Bray. Material was ordered so the ladies can make aprons, dresses, and pot holders for the Spring Sale. It was decided to hold one business meeting a month, and one other meeting if needed.

On December 26, 1958, Marion Crow Shoe and Joseph Yellow Wings were married in the chapel of Sacred Heart Indian Residential School.

A shower was held in the community hall on January 26 in honour of Mr. and Mrs. Joseph Yellow Wings. Mrs. Yellow Wings, nee Marion Crow Shoe, is a graduate of St. Cyprian's. Games were played under the supervision of Evelyn Crow Shoe, and there was dancing. Lunch was served to 80 visitors by the senior girls of the school. Then the happy couple were presented with many useful and lovely gifts.

A wedding took place in St. Cyprian's Church, Saturday, January 31 between Margaret Rose Crow Shoe of this reserve and Hector Jackson of Saddle Lake.

The Peigan W.A. held a shower in honour of Mrs. Hector Jackson at the home of Mrs. Joe Crow Shoe. She received many lovely and useful gifts for her home.

Joe Crow Shoe, Sr., Roy Cross Child, Jim Small Legs, Matthew One Owl, and Ben Many Guns are away working at Waterton Lakes, clearing brush and trees where a new highway to Chief Mountain will be built.

Four local boys, Henry Potts, Thomas Yellow Horn, Walter Smith, and Floyd Smith are in Edmonton taking a 10-week course in carpentry provided by the provincial government.

A large delegation of Indians attended the two-day agricultural meeting in the community hall in Brocket recently. Visitors from all the reserves in Alberta were here. Guest speakers were from Pincher Creek, Edmonton, and the various reserves.

Work started February 20 preparing poles, etc. to put electricity into the Indian homes in the Moccasin Flats area of the village of Brocket.

New babies since our last newsletter are: Marlene and Janet Jackson, daughters of Margaret and Hector Jackson; Evelyn Gladys, daughter of Elsie and John Prairie Chicken; Cary Lee, son of Rose North Peigan.

Sam Provost died December 13, 1958, (just after we printed our Christmas paper.) Sincere sympathy goes to his wife Maggie and the family from everyone at the school who knew him.

WELL DID YOU EVER! (reasons for not attending church – or the movies)
- When I go they always ask me for money.
- I went a few times, but no one spoke to me. Those who go there aren't very friendly.
- The person in charge never calls on me, so I won't go.
- I just can't sit still for so long.
- I don't always agree with what I see and hear.
- I don't like the kind of music they have.
- I went so much when I was a child, I've had enough of that stuff.

OUR SCHOOL CHAPEL, by the Reverend Stanger, Principal
The Anglican Newsletter, Easter, 1959

I want to tell you something about the activities in connection with our school chapel.

Each morning, Monday through Friday, we gather in the chapel to worship God. Pupils from grade three through grade eight have *Books of Common Prayer* with the hymn book included. In this way the children learn to use their prayer books as we join in the service of worship. We open these services with a hymn and then turn to one of the services suited to our needs, such as portions of *Morning Prayer, Service for Children, Prayers To Be Used In Families*, portions of *The Litany*, the *Service for Missions*, and *The Catechism*. At this assembly we have a reading of scripture or a story. The service lasts about twenty minutes so that even the youngest members of our school family can be attentive.

Pupils may go home every second weekend, so on the weekends they remain at school we have a special chapel service on Sunday afternoon. These services include object sermons. The children have learned such lessons as Christian worth, from salt; Christian abilities, from coal; and correcting mistakes in life, from an eraser.

Each Friday afternoon, pupils join their teachers in the chapel for fifteen minutes. This climaxes their week's activities in religious education.

Twice a month moving pictures in color, and with sound, are shown depicting the life of Jesus Christ. Holy Communion is celebrated in the chapel for staff members and for confirmed pupils.

SHOWERS (but no clouds!), by Kenneth Yellow Horn, *grade five, as submitted to The Anglican Newsletter, Easter, 1959*

During the Christmas holidays the boys' old bathroom was made into a shower room. There are four showers all in a row. There is a new cement floor with a long cement block all across the room that stops the water flowing all over the room. There is a new green wall halfway up. The top half of the wall and the ceiling are painted white.

The boys like to shower. It only takes half the time that bathing in the old tubs did. We think we are lucky to have showers.

NEW FLOOR IN BOYS' PLAYROOM, by Arnold Crazy Boy, *grade 8*

On January 10, Mr. McKinnon, contractor, finished laying the linoleum tiles in the boys' playroom. There is a checkerboard in the design on one side, and on the other side there is a hopscotch. The rest of the floor is grey tile with colored dots on it. It sure looks nice. When visitors come they all say, "My, what a nice floor the boys have!"

TOY STORE, by Miss How

On Friday, January 16, the junior classroom had their annual Toy Store.

All the children brought toys or games with prices marked on them. Each child was given forty-five cents in play money. Louisa, Ruby, and Billy were the storekeepers. The children went to the toy store in turn, bought the toys they wanted, and played with them for the rest of the day. Everyone enjoyed it very much.

W.A. ANNUAL MEETING HELD, by Miss How, secretary
as submitted to The Anglican Newsletter, Easter, 1959

The St. Cyprian School Women's Auxiliary held its annual meeting on Jan. 18 in the principal's apartment. The meeting opened with a short service of dedication.

After the minutes of the last meeting were read, reports were given by the treasurer. The president noted that 1958 had been a successful year for such a small group: eighteen meetings were held; jewelry was made to raise money; Japan was studied; eighteen layettes were given to Indian mothers on the reserve; financial obligations were met; and a corporate service of communion was held.

Voted back into office were Mrs. Stanger, president; Miss How, secretary; Mrs. Doolittle, treasurer. Plans for 1959 include the assembling of more baby bundles; the making of felt Christmas stockings for the girls in the school; reading the Canadian Social Service study book *He Cares*; a private study of details about the books of the Bible; and contributing to the United Pledge Fund. Plans were made for a *World Day of Prayer* service which will include the boys and girls of the school.

Light refreshments were served and recordings of familiar hymns were enjoyed. The president closed the meeting with prayer.

SHARON CROW SHOE IS NAMED "CHIEF STUDENT COUNCILLOR"

Four Councillors Elected

On Monday, January 26, all the pupils met in the junior classroom to elect a Student Council. The council has five members: a chief councillor, and two councillors from each classroom. Elected was chief councillor, Sharon Crow Shoe, and the councillors elected were Joe Crow Shoe, Ruby Crow Shoe, Hazel Weasel Bear, and Robert Crow Shoe.

The duties of the councillors are 1) to line up the pupils at recess and lead them to the classroom. 2) to assist the pupils, generally, in obeying the rules. 3) to act as monitors during school hours. Each councillor wears a blue band on the arm, and the chief councillor wears a red band.

SQUIRES ADVANCE, by L. Stanger, leader
as printed in The Anglican Newsletter, Easter, 1959

Fourteen squires of this school's Church Boys' League received new crests at the meeting on January 25:

Breastplate of Righteousness: Billy North Peigan, Robert Crow Shoe

Shield of Faith: Melvin Iron Shirt, Ronald Morning Bull

Helmet of Salvation: Gerald Crazy Boy, Gerald Crow Shoe, Kenneth Yellow Horn, Sam Born With A Tooth, John Stanger, Clifford Crow Shoe, Walter Crow Shoe, Woodrow North Peigan, George Weasel Bear and Arnold Crazy Boy.

At this meeting *the keeper of the purse* received a receipt from the Dominion Treasurer acknowledging payment by the group of their 58-59 fees, chapter renewal, and donations to the thank-offering and pledge fund.

The game played provided a lot of laughs; it was called *The Boiler Burst*.

The eighth chapter of *Invisible Armour*, the year's study book, was read and discussed, and then the meeting ended with the closing service.

SMILE:

Chief Big Screeching Train Whistle: "Judge, I want you to give me a shorter name."

Judge: "You mean shorter than *Big Screeching Train Whistle?* What do you have in mind?"

Chief: "*Toots!*"

POEMS ABOUT SCHOOL PETS
from the The Anglican Newsletter, Easter, 1959

Our Little Honey

Honey Stanger is my friend,
His tail is short and stout.
When he goes out, he will not stop
Until he's tired out.
(*by John Stanger*)

Honey is a nice young pup -
He is fat and brown,
His ears are soft and smooth and long,
His tail wags up and down.
(*by Sandra North Peigan*)

Honey, the cute and crazy dog,
Is sniffing at his bed.
He sniffs around at the kitchen door
When ready to be fed.
(*by Mildred Crow Shoe*)

We have a dog, his name is Honey
Who sometimes is so very funny.
He's always acting like a clown -
Jumping up and jumping down.
(*by Sam Born With A Tooth*)

Honey Stanger is our friend,
Round and fat is he.
Jumping in the snow each time,
Happy, merry, as a bee.
(by Hazel Weasel Bear)

. . .

Cats, Cats! We Have Lots Of Cats.

There are many cats at this school,
Some are white and some are grey.
They walk around the big red barn,
And catch the mice, we pray.
(by Betty Red Young Man)

Princess was born in the pig-house last year,
She is as white as the snow.
She's the cat that is kind of fat,
I like her the best, I know.
(by Judy Stanger)

There are lots of different cats
At this school of ours,
Sometimes they are seen to play
Among the garden flowers.
(by Mary Born With A Tooth)

Cute kittens are my very best -
When they see me, they will jump.
They're oh so nice, but little pests
All scampering 'round the stump.
(*by Patsy Yellow Horn*)

Cats are many around the school,
Some are big and some are small.
Every morning they are fed,
Then they cuddle like a ball.
(*by George Weasel Bear*)

My Life's Story Thus Far, *by Mrs. McGuffie, teacher*

as printed in The Anglican Newsletter, Easter, 1959

Until my eighteenth birthday I lived in Africa, going to a residential school in Port Elizabeth, and then for two years to the Teachers' Training College in Cape Town. As my home was on a farm in the mountainous region called the Great Karroo[4], my holidays were often spent helping in the wool-sheds, or coaxing notoriously-bad goat mothers to nurse their kids. Our eyes were always on the clouds, because when a thunderstorm came everyone rushed outside, supremely happy. Armed with spades, we would direct the water onto our parched gardens and cultivated fields.

From this land of drought, I went for two years more training at the International College for Physical Training in Denmark. There, I lived with students of thirteen different nationalities, and was filled with a desire to see their homelands. During the holidays, I was able to visit many European countries. Then it

---

[4] *The Great Karoo is an area of more than 400,000 square kilometers of dry thirsty land, a boundless and mysterious area that is extremely hot in summer and extremely cold in winter.*

was home to Africa again, to teach in various centers, including Johanesburg, the City of Gold.

Children and adults alike, in the warm climate of Africa, spend most of their lives out-of-doors. School starts at 7 a.m. and ends at 12:45 p.m. During the summer, the afternoons are spent swimming, playing tennis or cricket, and often end with supper in the open. In winter, ground hockey, net ball and rugby are added to the list of games.

After I married, I lived on a farm for eight years in the Kalahari desert. Life was tough, because we were always battling droughts, floods, locusts or hailstorms. These hazards, together with minor incidents with snakes and insects, gave colour to our lives, while a continuous challenge to survive saved us from monotony and boredom.

In 1933, when every possible disaster hit us in twelve months, we moved to Swaziland on the east side of the continent. Here in a region of plentiful summer rainfall, we settled down to a life of easier farming. However, there was far more excitement caused by hippos, snakes, crocodiles, and lions. In this area, the Africans were still isolated from the civilization of the west and, despite their primitive way of living, they were a simple and happy people.

World War Two caught up with us, and my husband left for Cairo, and I took over the running of the 36,000 acre farm. The Africans had promised their help, so together we battled for two years with little items like worms in sheep and calves, and cutworms in the soil. Ticks small and red, ticks large and blue, haunted our lives - not to mention the blowflies whose maggots devoured our sheep alive. Then came news that my husband had died at Tobruk. No time to think against the clamouring needs of an enormous farm, and so my life there continued until somebody was found to take over from me.

From Southern Rhodesia came an urgent letter asking me to teach again, so back to the lights of towns and civilization my daughter and I went. Here on a holiday safari trip, I was thrown from a horse, and not knowing I had a cracked hip and two broken vertebrae, I walked fifty miles propped on two sticks. In order not to hold up the party, I set out ahead each morning with an old African guide armed only with an assagai[5]. One day, coming around a headland, we met a lion stalking some buck. Unable to run, I had to stand still and hope for the best. The buck, scenting us, started to run; the lion, intent on its prey, loped after them, leaving us to recover from shock. After this, for a couple years, I acted as general assistant to two doctor friends.

My daughter now decided she wanted to train to become a physiotherapist. So after fourteen days on the sea, we reached battle-scarred England. For me, there were more years of teaching in a small private school near London. With long summer holidays spent wandering through Norway, Sweden, Austria, Yugoslavia, Holland and Spain, ten years seemed to pass in a flash.

Having now become grandma to a Canadian grandchild, it seemed time to become acquainted more closely with the New World. So here I am, to learn from your way of life and, in return, I hope to try and help you understand the life and problems of people across the seas.

---

5 *Assegai or assagai is a light spear or lance with a short shaft and a long blade for close combat.*

AN EASTER THOUGHT, by the Reverend Stanger, Principal
as taken from The Anglican Newsletter, Easter, 1959

With the coming of Easter, our spirits are awakened to the Divine Plan of the renewal of all that is good. Evil may cloud life for a season, but it will not endure. This is what we call hope.

To the followers of Jesus, who had found in Him a cause for awakened hope, the days before His crucifixion must have been terrible indeed. With the crucifixion would come the agonizing illusion that perhaps evil would endure; perhaps what the Nazarene taught and lived were doomed in the face of the powers of evil. But consider then the visit by Mary Magdalene to the sepulcher early in the morning to find the stone no longer blocking the entrance to the tomb, and the tomb empty. Then, the stranger on the road to Emmaus; the disciples in the room; the appearance of Jesus, and His words, "Why are ye troubled? Behold, my hands and my feet, that it is I myself."

Truly, Easter is a season for joy and for hope. He has given us power to become children of God. Let us take Him into our lives and learn of Him. It is by Him, we are raised from sin to life, and He is that light of life.

May the grace of our Lord Jesus Christ be with us all evermore.

OUR SCHOOL SONG
from The Anglican Newsletter, June, 1959

We are the pupil of St. Cyprian's
Our school is our hope and pride.
Our aim is to be good citizens,
The glory of the Peigan tribe.

We come back each year to old St. Cyprian's
To learn to do as we should.
We'll be good sports if we win or lose,
And stand for what is right and good.

We are the pupils of St. Cyprian's
Our school is our hope and pride.
Our aim is to be good citizens,
The glory of the Peigan tribe.

. . .

THE SUNBEAMS
as taken from The Anglican Newsletter, June, 1959

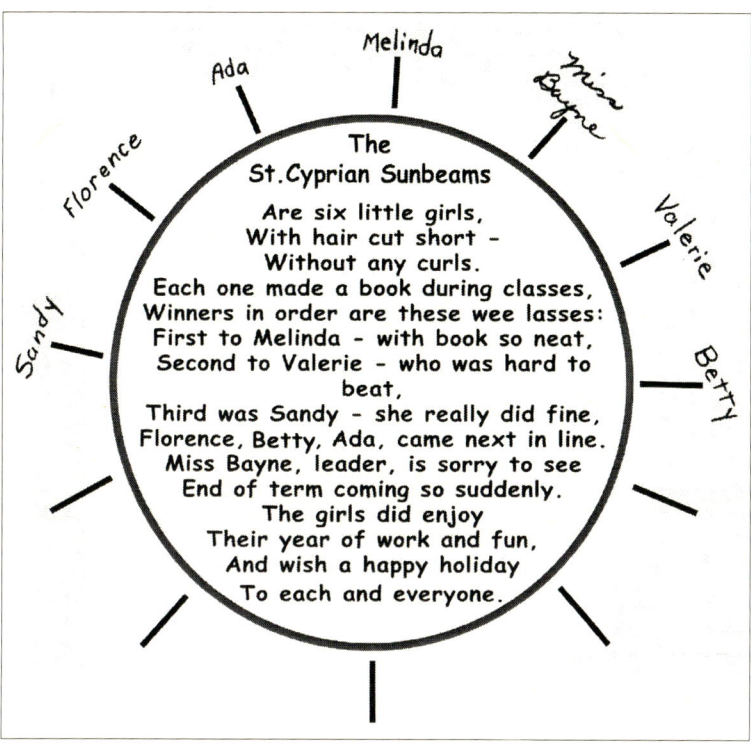

THE SCHOOL COUNCIL, by Mildred Crow Shoe
as printed in The Anglican Newsletter, June, 1959

To assist Sharon Crow Shoe, *Chief Councillor*, during the month of March the students elected councillors: Woodrow North Peigan, Mildred Crow Shoe, Gordon Buffalo, and Donna Crow Shoe.

For April, the councillors elected were Walter Crow Shoe, Patsy Yellow Horn, Harvey Plain Eagle, and Louisa Crow Shoe.

For May, the elected councillors were Joe Crow Shoe and Sandra North Peigan from the senior classroom; Vernon Morning Bull and Hazel Crazy Boy from the junior classroom.

There were no councillors elected for June.

At the second election, the senior classroom sent in their suggestions for rules which they thought would help in case of a fire. The suggestions were voted on, and the following four adopted:

1) Stand quietly at attention when in line.
2) Do not talk on the stairs.
3) Walk two steps behind the person in front of you.
4) Always speak English in an emergency.

After each new election we have a meeting, and a party. The teachers see that every month Chief Sharon Crow Shoe gets one dollar, and that each of the councillors get fifty cents. One fifth of it is supposed to go into our school bank. This money is to be used for anything the councillors decide will be for the good of everyone in the school.

PICNIC, PRESENTATIONS, AND BRAND NEW KNIGHTS
as written in The Anglican Newsletter, June, 1959

Sunday, June 7, a picnic supper was had by all the groups to close off activities for the 58-59 term. Earlier the same day nine members of the *Church Boys League* were made *Knights* during a special service in the chapel. All groups and the leaders were in uniform. The new Knights are George Weasel Bear, Woodrow North Peigan, Kenneth Yellow Horn, Gerald Crow Shoe, Walter Crow Shoe, Sam Born, John Stanger, Ronald Morning

Bull, and Clifford Crow Shoe. They were presented with New Testaments.

The G.A. president, Mildred Crow Shoe, took the opportunity of presenting to Sharon Crow Shoe a framed felt shield to which was attached all the badges and chevrons earned in her years in the G.A. Sharon was graduated last June, but returned to gain one more grade this year. When the G.A. president, on behalf of all members, expressed good wishes to Sharon she was in fact saying exactly what everyone at the school wishes for Sharon.

G.A. Members: Sharon, Annabelle, Sandra, Mildred, Hazel, Patsy
Leader: Miss Bray
Activities:

> Handicrafts, knitting and cooking were done
> By the G.A. of St. Cyprian - and badges were won
> By all six girls, and they enjoyed the time
> Spent in learning things of many kinds.
>
> Visitors were welcomed to some of the meetings,
> The girls also received a lot of greetings.
> As the term for 1959 ends
> We'd like to say goodbye to our friends.
>
> Thanks very much for the help given by all
> Have a good holiday; we'll see you next fall.

MISS HOW WRITES FROM KILLARNEY, IRELAND
letter dated June 2, 1959

"Our polar flight was very thrilling. We flew over Canada at about 250 miles per hour, at 15,000 feet up. At that speed it took us about twelve hours to reach the Atlantic Ocean. We flew over Hudson Bay, and stopped at Frobisher Bay on Baffin Island to refuel.

"Across the Atlantic and over Greenland we flew above the clouds. However, the next afternoon we saw the Hebrides, Scotland, and Holland. After a short stop at Amsterdam, we flew to London.

"Since then we've been on the go all the time. We've seen so many interesting places and done so many different things, it would take pages to tell about them. So I'll just tell you what I did today.

"At 10:30 a.m. we got into Irish jaunting cars, and drove for about five miles to the mountains. Then we got into a pony trap and went through a mountain pass (about 7 1/2 miles). This part took over two hours. We had lunch at the head of the three Killarney lakes. Then we got into a big row boat, and were rowed down the three lakes. We saw a castle, the ruins of an old monastery, miles of beautiful scenery, and at last we saw the jaunting cars ready to take us back to our hotel. We reached the hotel about 6 p.m. very tired, sunburned, and hungry.

"Next we go on a tour around England and Scotland. I'm taking plenty of moving pictures, so you'll be able to see them next fall."

SPRING ON THE PRAIRIE

by Judith Stanger, grade 6,
as printed in The Anglican Newsletter, June 1959

It was lovely out this morning,
As the sun rose up to view,
The meadowlarks were singing,
Good morning, good morning to you.

The little green wheat sprouts are turning,
Their little green heads to the sun,
Mother Nature is spreading her dress of green
Spring has surely, surely begun.

Little white clouds across the sky,
Make pictures so clear and true,
Dandelions nod their heads in the breeze,
The calves all shout, "moo, moo!"

The blossoms upon the hillside
Begin to show their wear,
The meadows all are green now,
They show up everywhere.

As the sun sinks down behind the hill
Its daily journey done,
The stars come out to twinkle
At the end of a spring day's fun.

A breeze comes gently blowing
Night settles softly o'er the land,
Bringing peace to all the earth
And sleep to everyone.

SMILES:

Mom: Jimmy, sit down and tell me what your school grades are.

Jimmy: I can't sit down. I just told Pop what they were.

• • •

Clerk: Sir, there's a salesman outside with a bald head.

Boss: Tell him to go away. I've already got one.

RIDDLES

• Why did the little drop of ink cry?

Because his mother was in the pen and he didn't know how long the sentence would be.

• • •

• Why does an Indian wear feathers in his bonnet?

To keep his wigwam.

THE HUSTLERS AND THE RANGERS, by George Weasel Bear, grade eight, *as printed in The Anglican Newsletter, June, 1959*

In April all the pupils were divided into two groups. After suggestions and voting, the two groups are *The Rangers* and *The Hustlers*. Then we decided to choose colours - red for the Rangers and green for the Hustlers.

We have played many games of softball in which *The Rangers* won five games and *The Hustlers* two games. There was a mixed team match between the two groups, which ended in a draw. A spelling competition was held every week in the senior classroom with *The Rangers* winning. There was very little difference between the teams, and the spelling in our classroom has improved a lot. In the junior classroom *The Hustlers* came out on top.

THE RANGERS

George Weasel Bear, Captain
Annabelle Buffalo, Captain
Mildred Crow Shoe
Patsy Yellow Horn
Judith Stanger
Carolyn Yellow Horn
Woodrow North Peigan
Clifford Crow Shoe
Ronald Morning Bull
Eric North Peigan
Woodrow Crow Eagle
Leroy Black Eyes
Robert Crow Shoe
Gordon Buffalo
Vernon Morning Bull
Conrad Big Bull

THE HUSTLERS

Joe Crow Shoe, Captain
Sharon Crow Shoe, Captain
Hazel Weasel Bear
Sandra North Peigan
Mary Born With A Tooth
Betty Red Young Man
John Stanger
Gerald Crow Shoe
Melvin Iron Shirt
Walter Crow Shoe
Sammy Born With A Tooth
Kenneth Yellow Horn
Oliver Crow Eagle
Gerald Crazy Boy
Harvey Plain Eagle
Billy North Peigan

Bryon Yellow Horn
Louis Crow Eagle
Howard One Owl
Donna Crow Shoe
Glennis Crow Shoe
Louisa Crow Shoe
Valerie Crow Shoe
Hazel Crazy Boy
Arnold Crazy Boy
Linda Yellow Horn
Linda North Peigan
Ada Buffalo
Betty Crazy Boy

Melvin Plain Eagle
Jeffrey Crow Shoe
Reggie Crow Shoe
Darryll Crow Shoe
Douglas Yellow Horn
Ruby Crow Shoe
Diane North Peigan
Doreen Weasel Bear
Florence Weasel Bear
Sandy Big Bull
Melinda Crow Eagle
Corrine Iron Shirt
Barbara Crow Shoe
Roberta Iron Shirt
Eric Crow Shoe

RANGERS BATTLE CRY

Up the Rangers into battle,
Beat that Hustler team.
Never weaken, never falter,
Lift your head and scream
R a n g e r s! R a n g e r s!
We are the stronger team!

HUSTLERS BATTLE CRY

Young Hustlers, Young Hustlers,
Young Hustlers are we.
For playing hard, and playing fair
We'll beat all we see.
There's a run there for you,
And a point here for me,
It all adds to a score
Which spells v i c t o r y!

A PICNIC BY THE SPRING, by Hazel Weasel Bear, grade 6,
as printed in The Anglican Newsletter, June, 1959

At last the day arrived. Unfortunately it wasn't a pleasant day, because the weather was a bit cold and windy for a picnic.

On Saturday morning Mildred, Annabelle, Patsy, Helen, and I cut sandwiches, while the boys and girls played outside.

Helen Weasel Bear and Miss Bray wondered if we really should have the picnic because it was cold, but the sun came out and they decided it would be all right.

Miss Bray sent Mildred and me over to Marie's place to get Francis to take the lunch, ourselves, and the smaller children over to the spring. Helen had started out with some of the older girls and boys who wanted to fish.

When we got there, Helen and her lot had arrived, and we all split up and did what we wished. Mrs. McGuffie and the senior girls went looking for flowers. The senior boys started fishing, and the others played games with Miss Bray and Helen.

About noon we ate our lunch. Louisa, Glennis, and Helen gave out the prunes, raw carrots, sandwiches, and the drink.

After lunch the senior girls took Mrs. McGuffie to see Mildred's little baby cousin.

Then we had to return to the school. The other children went ahead and got back before we did. Everyone was blown along very fast by the wind. On the way we found a caterpillar which we thought was horrible to pick up. We all returned safe and sound, cold but happy.

WHAT SHALL I DO WITH MY LIFE? by L. Stanger
as written in The St. Cyprian's Newsletter, 1959,

Throughout Canada, today, many young people are thinking, *what shall I do with my life?* Others have already started out on some path which they hope will take them all the way to their desired goals - if they can manage to get over the rough spots along the way. Yes, each path has a few bumps, but it is a courageous young adult who will not be discouraged; it is a steadfast young adult who will succeed and become an inspiration for others.

We have here at *St. Cyprian's* such an inspiration. We have Miss Evelyn Crow Shoe.

Evelyn was born at Brocket on June 4, 1936, the first of Joe and Josephine Crow Shoe's large family, and she attended this school until her sixteenth birthday. After graduation, and after staying at home for a year, she did housework for three months at a farm near Fishburn.

When Evelyn returned to this school as a staff member, she was a laundry assistant. Three years later she was in charge of the laundry and, using part of her holidays, she took a course in recreational leadership at Red Deer, Alberta. Then she went back for a refresher course, and encouraged one of her brothers to begin the course as well..

This training has been beneficial not only to Miss Crow Shoe, but to our school and the community. She leads physical training, sports, and handicrafts with the children in the school on a regular basis and, with her brother's help, she carries on various recreational activities in the village of Brocket.

This school term, Miss Crow Shoe assumed the role of general assistant - in addition to her recreational work. As general assistant, she supervises the boys one day each week and the girls another day - when the supervisors have a day off. A third day each week she relieves the cook, and prepares meals for seventy-five people. This is one of her favourite jobs, she says.

Nevertheless, Evelyn is interested in traveling, and has some long-term goals. She has been thinking she would like further training in missionary work, with an eye to becoming a Sunday school van worker, or something of that sort.

Miss Crow Shoe has not only proven herself capable in a wide range of work situations, but she is a pleasure to have here at *St. Cyprian's*, whether working, or playing softball, skating, or dancing. Indeed, Evelyn should be proud of her talents, her achievements, and her vision.

We are very proud of Miss Evelyn Crow Shoe, and we appreciate the examples of courage, steadfastness, joy of living, and the inspiration she gives to all those around her - especially our young people as they ponder the question, "What shall I do with my life?"

LOCAL NEWS, by E. Bray
as printed in The Anglican Newsletter, June 1959

The Peigan W.A. have held several rummage sales and a very successful parcel post table. The ladies would like to take this opportunity of saying thank you to all who have helped during the year. The last meeting of this season is to be at the new home of Mrs. Lily Crow Shoe this month.

A Medicine Pipe Dance was held in Brocket beside the tepee of Mrs. Joe Buffalo on June 2.

On May 10 there was a fire in Brocket. The community hall was a complete loss. Two young men from the reserve lost their lives as a result - Dennis Muggins and Andrew Stump. Condolences to the families of these two men.

A car accident about the middle of May sent Hilda Big Swan to hospital in Lethbridge with a fractured skull.

Evelyn Crow Shoe is now a girls' supervisor at the Old Sun Indian School, Gleichen.

Miss How is on a trip to Europe. Several cards have been received from London telling us she is having a wonderful time.

Small boys playing with a loaded gun resulted in the death of five-year-old Bobby Earl Crow Eagle on June 3. Our sincere sympathy to the family.

Joe Crow Shoe, Sr. attended the Laymen's Conference at Banff in April.

Eleanor Knowlton will be graduating from Alberta College this term.

Marie Crow Shoe is working three days a week at the school.

Margaret Water Chief, nee Big Bull, from Gleichen is working at the school for the month of June.

New babies since our Easter Newsletter: A girl to Jerry and Rose Potts.

Boys to Mona and Jackie Crow Shoe; to Nancy and Archie Big Swan; and to Jane and Pete Crow Eagle. Congratulations!

Greetings to Jim Morning Bull who is progressing favourably at the Charles Camsell Hospital, and to Ambrose Two Chief, a patient in a Calgary hospital.

Congratulations to Sharon Crow Shoe, George Weasel Bear, and Joseph Crow Shoe. They will be graduated from St. Cyprian's the end of June. They have finished grade eight, and they hope to go on to The Alberta College, in Edmonton, next fall.

SPORTS DAY, Tuesday, June 16, 1959

The sports day was held on the boys' playground. The weather was fine and calm, and everyone enjoyed themselves. A treat of hot-dogs and fruit punch served at the intermission certainly added to the success of the occasion.

Mr. Stanger, Miss Watson, and Miss Bayne acted as judges. Miss Bray was the recorder, and Mrs. McGuffie was the starter. Our thanks go to Mr. Brown for his cooperation in preparing the field and his assistance during the afternoon.

The competitors were divided into seven groups according to age and sex, and then competed for points - each for their particular group. At the end of the day *The Rangers* were the victors by 24 points.

The results were as follows:

Flat Race

Group	Name	Team	Place	Points
Group A	George Weasel Bear	Ranger	1st	5
	Ronald Morning Bull	Ranger	2nd	3
	Walter Crow Shoe	Hustler	3rd	1
Group B	Robert Crow Shoe	Ranger	1st	5
	Billy North Peigan	Hustler	2nd	3
	Melvin Iron Shirt	Hustler	3rd	1
Group C	Douglas Yellow Horn	Hustler	1st	5
	Darryll Crow Shoe	Hustler	2nd	3
	Melvin Plain Eagle	Hustler	3rd	1
Group D	Mildred Crow Shoe	Ranger	1st	5
	Patsy Yellow Horn	Ranger	2nd	3
	Hazel Weasel Bear	Hustler	3rd	1
Group E	Judith Stanger	Ranger	1st	5
	Betty Red Young Man	Hustler	2nd	3
	Carolyn Yellow Horn	Ranger	3rd	1
Group F	Diane North Peigan	Hustler	1st	5
	Glennis Crow Shoe	Ranger	2nd	3
	Mary Born With A Tooth	Hustler	3rd	1

Group G	Bryan Yellow Horn	Ranger	1st	5
	Reggie Crow Shoe	Hustler	2nd	3
	Howard One Owl	Ranger	3rd	1

High Jump

				Points
Group A	George Weasel Bear (4ft. 6in.)	Ranger	1st	5
	Ronald Morning Bull	Ranger	2nd	3
	Walter Crow Show	Hustler	3rd	1
Group B	Robert Crow Shoe	Ranger	1st	5
	Billy North Peigan	Hustler	2nd	3
	Melvin Iron Shirt	Hustler	3rd	1
Group C	John Stanger	Hustler	1st	5
	Eric Crow Shoe	Hustler	2nd	3
Group D/E	Sharon Crow Shoe	Hustler	1st	4
	Carolyn Yellow Horn	Ranger	1st	4
	Mildred Crow Shoe	Ranger	3rd	1

Softball Throw

				Points
Group A/B	Joe Crow Shoe	Hustler	1st	5
	George Weasel Bear	Ranger	2nd	3
	Woodrow North Peigan	Ranger	3rd	1

Broad Jump

				Points
Group A	George Weasel Bear	Ranger	1st	5
	Woodrow North Peigan	Ranger	2nd	3
	Walter Crow Shoe	Hustler	3rd	1
Group B	Melvin Iron Shirt	Hustler	1st	5
	Robert Crow Shoe	Ranger	2nd	3
	Billy North Peigan	Hustler	3rd	1

Potato Race

				Points
Group C	John Stanger	Hustler	1st	5
	Darryll Crow Shoe	Hustler	2nd	3
	Douglas Yellow Horn	Hustler	3rd	1

Group D	Mildred Crow Shoe	Ranger	1st	5
	Sharon Crow Shoe	Hustler	2nd	3
	Hazel Weasel Bear	Hustler	3rd	1
Group F	Donna Crow Shoe	Ranger	1st	5
	Glennis Crow Shoe	Ranger	2nd	3
	Mary Born With A Tooth	Hustler	3rd	1
Group G	Reggie Crow Shoe	Hustler	1st	5
	Bryan Yellow Horn	Ranger	2nd	3
	Howard One Owl	Ranger	3rd	1

Sack Race Points

Group B	Sam Born With A Tooth	Hustler	1st	5
	Robert Crow Shoe	Ranger	2nd	3
	Billy North Peigan	Hustler	3rd	1
Group C	Darryll Crow Shoe	Hustler	1st	5
	John Stanger	Hustler	2nd	3
	Douglas Yellow Horn	Hustler	3rd	1
Group D	Mildred Crow Shoe	Ranger	1st	5
	Sharon Crow Shoe	Hustler	2nd	3
	Patsy Yellow Horn	Ranger	3rd	1
Group E	Carolyn Yellow Horn	Ranger	1st	5
	Louisa Crow Shoe	Ranger	2nd	3
	Linda North Peigan	Ranger	3rd	1
Group F	Donna Crow Shoe	Ranger	1st	5
	Hazel Crazy Boy	Ranger	2nd	3
	Linda Yellow Horn	Ranger	3rd	1
Group G	Bryan Yellow Horn	Ranger	1st	5
	Reggie Crow Shoe	Hustler	2nd	3
	Jeffery Crow Shoe	Hustler	3rd	1

Egg & Spoon Race Points

Group G	Reggie Crow Shoe	Hustler	1st	5
	Florence Weasel Bear	Hustler	2nd	3
	Betty Crazy Boy	Ranger	3rd	1

Boys' Relay Race   Rangers   5
Girls' Relay Race   Rangers   5

Casualty List: Clifford Crow Shoe, a Ranger, sprained his ankle

OUR MAILBOX, by L. Stanger
as submitted to The Anglican Newsletter, June, 1959

We are delighted indeed to have received so many heartwarming letters from readers of *The Anglican Newsletter*. While it is impossible to share all of these letters with everyone, we can briefly note some of the comments, and indicate on a map of North America and Great Britain the various areas where those letters were written.

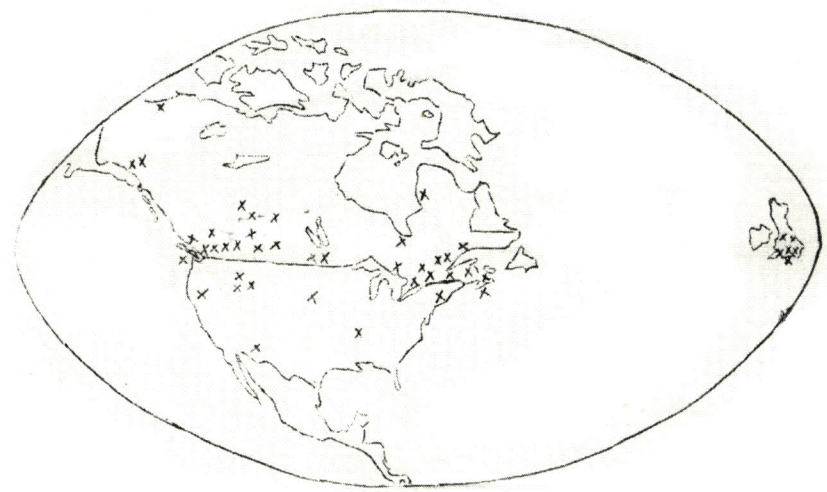

SOME COMMENTS

excerpts from some of those letters:

- Thanks for sharing your school paper with us.
- Congratulations on the success of *The Newsletter* and the good quality of the material published.
- I like to see the children's artistic efforts, and am very interested in good news of the ex-pupils, and their progress on, or off, the reserve.
- I shall be interested in future articles on "What Shall I Do With My Life?"

- All the J.A. girls were delighted with the articles, and were happy to be making gifts for the girls there . . . Keep 'em coming, please.
- The newsletters give me a pretty good picture of life there.
- I think the children have quite an active life there at St. Cyprian's.
- When I finish reading a newsletter, I pass it on to the leader of the Little Helpers who can make use of some of the material with her group.
- We have used the principal's messages at our W.A. meetings.
- We do enjoy the newsletters so much, and imagine you are kept very busy with all the children . . . the activities sound like fun.
- It is very nice that all children, grades one to eight are in it.
- I use the newsletters in my sermon.
- We like the drawings.
- We read it aloud at W.A. meetings.
- I look forward to the next issue . . . keep them coming.
- All my neighbours read the copy I receive.
- My son wastes no time getting at the activity page.
- I would like to read more about activities in the school chapel.
- What has happened to *Our Mr. Doolittle?* Does he not talk any more?
- It was great to hear about some of the pupils choosing to return to school beyond the required age of sixteen so they can complete grade eight and go on to high school or a community college.
- It is interesting to know that you have several of your school graduates now on staff there.
- So, the native school children are also into hula hoop!

A MESSAGE FROM YOUR PRINCIPAL, the Reverend C.T Stanger
as taken from The Anglican Newsletter, June, 1959

Once again a school year is coming to a close, and the summer holidays are drawing near, with an excitement that is felt throughout the school.

At this time I wish it were possible to thank each and every one who has contributed to the well-being of our school, everyone who has helped in any way to make St. Cyprian's a happy and productive place of learning. But because it is not possible to list everyone, it must suffice to name the present staff, the dedicated men and women who constantly go the extra mile. To them I extend my sincere thanks:

Our Maintenance Men: Mr. Doolittle and Mr. Brown

Our Supervisors: Miss Bray (boys) and Mrs. Doolittle (girls)

Our Cook: Mrs. Fidler

Our Kitchen Helper: Miss Weasel Bear

Our Seamstress: Miss Bayne

Our Matron: Mrs. Stanger

Our Teachers: Miss How and Mrs. McGuffie

Miss How is vacationing in Europe, but will be back here in September. During May and June, Miss Watson has taught the pupils of the junior classroom.

The only members of the present school personnel who anticipate leaving this summer are my wife and myself. We shall be moving to Ontario the first of August where I expect to enter the parish work of the church. Since I entered residential school work in 1951 - serving in the Yukon and here in southern Alberta - our two youngsters started *going to school* in the Yukon with the pupils of Chooutla, and they have enjoyed continuing on here with the boys and girls of St. Cyprian's. Therefore, this summer will be the start of a whole new journey for them, as well as it will be for their parents.

Our new place of residence has not been decided, but any mail will find us if sent in care of Mr. T. S. Harris, Beachburg, Ontario. We will certainly miss our large school family, but trust that God will bless each of you. On behalf of my family and myself, our very best wishes always.

The Stangers as they leave St. Cyprian's

HOME ON THE RANGE

Home On the Range has been sung everywhere for the last 140 years - in haylofts and in concert halls; in classrooms and in barracks; around pianos and around campfires . . . . Even though *Home On The Range* is a traditional cowboy song, it still speaks to those of us who rode the range in a Chevrolet.

When Dr. Brewster M. Higley published the poem, *My Western Home,* he could not have envisioned it as a popular song - but then Daniel E. Kelley supplied the music in 1873.

Some of the words from a few of the numerous original stanzas are:

Oh, give me a home, where the buffalo roam,
Where the deer and the antelope play;
Where seldom is heard a discouraging word,
And the skies are not cloudy all day.

>   **CHORUS**
>   Home, home on the range,
>   Where the deer and the antelope play;
>   Where seldom is heard a discouraging word,
>   And the skies are not cloudy all day.

Oh, I love these wild flowers in this dear land of ours;
The curlew I love to hear scream;
And I love the white rocks and the antelope flocks,
That graze on the mountain-tops green.

Oh, I would not exchange my home on the range,
Where the deer and the antelope play;
Where seldom is heard a discouraging word,
And the skies are not cloudy all day.

Down through the years stanzas have been added, deleted, and changed, but the sheer joy of singing it never changes. As an unofficial anthem of the west, *Home On The Range* makes everyone a westerner for a little while.

CHAPTER SEVEN

SCRAPBOOK

"A hundred years from now it won't matter what my bank account was, the sort of house I lived in, or the kind of car I drove. But the world may be different because I was important in the life of a child."

Forest E. Witcraft (1894-1967)
teacher and scout leader.

TO EVERYTHING THERE IS A SEASON *(Ecclesiastes 3: 1)*
by Laura, 2012

St. Cyprian's Indian Residential School was in operation for 35 years. During that time it offered two thousand children basic life skills, and the basic elementary education that was required for admission to high school or trade school; to join the military, or to follow some other chosen route on their way into adulthood.

Since residential school days, the Peigan Nation has continued to be made up of quiet and talented people who have never been afraid to try new ideas. They were the first band in Alberta to demand a vote in provincial elections, the first to assume administration of their own reserve, and the first to host *Indian Days* as a means of retraining and maintaining their native culture.

Today, the Peigan people continue to strive for self-determination and economic independence for both present and future generations. They have established employment ventures for their band members, and in 1986 they took control of their own education by building a high school on the reserve.

Visiting Brocket as tourists in 1978, my husband and my son found a fine new administrative building in Brocket and, venturing inside, they discovered that the administrator was a young man who had been a student at *St. Cyprian's Indian Residential School* during our tenure in the 1950s. He was Reggie Crow Shoe, a son of Joe and Josephine who are featured elsewhere in this scrapbook section. More recently, I learned that the same Reg Crow Shoe had been made Chief Crow Shoe.

News like that made me remember many of the other students, and I would have loved to look into a crystal ball to see what they were doing as adults. But since I didn't have a crystal ball, I decided to read again their stories, and enjoy again their artwork - just as we had printed it in our school newspapers when we were all together during the period 1956 - 1959.

Those fragile but precious newsletters told me what some of the pupils had hoped to do with their lives. However, even if various different paths were taken after leaving *St. Cyprian's*, it is my sincere wish that now - as today's senior citizens - they can look back on lives that have made them proud. I hope, also, that they can look back even farther to school days that prompt good memories of *St. Cyprian's Indian Residential School*.

THE OLD MAN AND THE OLD WOMAN
by Laura

Joe Crow Shoe
The Indian in headdress is Joe Crow Shoe, Sr.

The old man, Joe, died October 29, 1999 at age 93. The old woman, Josephine, died Jan 31, 2002 at age 84. In their native culture, being named *old man and old woman* is a great honour. In fact, it is the highest religious honour that the Blackfoot Confederacy can bestow on a couple.

I am glad to have known Joe and Josephine Crow Shoe (or *Crowshoe*). They were neighbors and, in a way, they were colleagues in the late 1950s. That was long before I learned how famous they were destined to become.

Joe and Josephine had about a dozen children as well as some adopted children, and they chose to send those of elementary school age to the residential school where my husband and I were working in the 1950s, and where our own two children attended classes. Joe was a sub chief; he was also a lay-reader who assisted in the little Anglican church in the village of Brocket. Thus, their family home and church were only four miles from the residential school.

As I look at pictures of Joe and Josephine, my memories take me back fifty-six years. Back to the Peigan Indian Reserve in Alberta; back to St. Cyprian's Indian Residential School when that was our home.

Christmas, 1956, was our first Christmas at St. Cyprian's, and it was extra special because my parents and my aunt came west to visit us, and they arrived in time to enjoy the Christmas concert put on in the village by our school staff and pupils. Afterwards, many of the residential children went home to be with their parents, and we were able to enjoy some quality time with mine.

Shortly before Mom and Dad were scheduled to leave, we invited Joe and Josephine over to our apartment for a visit. When their daughter, Evelyn, one of our staff members, arrived wearing her beautiful native outfit, and when Joe arrived carrying his handcrafted rawhide native drum, we felt sure the evening was going to be memorable.

Evelyn in costume with her parents and mine.

Joe and my dad had something in common. Joe was a band councillor on the Peigan Reserve and my dad was a councillor in the township where he lived. In about two minutes they were friends. They talked and talked and, with Joe's permission, Dad soon got busy recording their conversation on his brand new tape recorder. Of course that picked up all the other chit-chat going on in the room as well. When Dad played-back his recording for all to hear, the fun really began. Our visitors giggled with delight, but they couldn't quite believe they were hearing their own voices coming from Dad's magic box in the corner of the room.

The Stangers and their guests - Evelyn, Josephine and Joe Crow Shoe, Christmas 1956

Next came the moment when we non-aborigines were treated to some aboriginal magic. Joe beat his drum while his family chanted and gave us a dance demonstration. That looked like fun, so we paleface novices simply had to get into the act. Thus, the people who knew what they were doing partnered with those who didn't, and our dance lesson began. Getting our tongues around the unfamiliar chants was impossible, so we concentrated on our feet. Trying to make them move to the rhythm was enough of a challenge - one that my dad escaped.

What was Dad doing? Well, with his other new toy, he was making a movie! A movie of us all doubled over in gales of laughter. It is surprising that our guests didn't cry as we reduced their captivating dance to a dreadful mess, but they laughed right along with us. It was great fun! It was also perfectly clear which dancers would *never* perform at an *Indian Days* festival.

Our evening wound down with us all sitting around the dining room table, as our guests helped us with the Blackfoot words for sandwich, cake, ice cream, and coffee. We also learned that *Oki* meant *hello*. Aunt Nina was very good at getting her tongue around native words - perhaps because she and her husband had farmed in Saskatchewan many years before.

Just before saying goodnight, Joe presented Dad with his drum as a token of appreciation for their time together. For my dad, that sincere gesture of friendship was his personal moment of magic. Joe's drum was taken back to Ontario and hung above the fireplace in Dad's den. There the story of the drum was told and re-told to friends and family. Indeed, Dad continued telling it as long as he lived, and afterwards I told it to the curator of a museum in Pembroke who was delighted to accept the handmade Peigan drum - a drum that had been important to both a First Nations municipal councillor in Alberta and a non-native one in Ontario.

Today, thanks to newspaper clippings and research, I know much more about Joe and Josephine than I did away back in the 1950s. I know that *the old man and the old woman* left very big footprints in the sands of time for those brave enough to follow.

With compassion, Joe and Josephine worked for peace in their own lives and in their community. Actually, they were ambassadors of peace and goodwill well-beyond the borders of Canada. For example, they traveled to places such as Mexico, New Zealand, China....

Joe and Josephine received the *Order of Canada*, a *National Aboriginal Achievement Award*, and a *Citation of Citizenship from the Government of Canada*. Joe received *two honorary doctorates*: one in Law from the University of Calgary, and one in Humanities from the University of Montana. Joe and Josephine also received numerous documents expressing gratitude for their work on the first-ever Blackfoot language dictionary, and included among those was one from the University of Calgary and one from the University of Lethbridge.

Josephine has been quoted as saying, *Just as the sun dance requires a man and a woman together as head of their religious practice, neither man nor woman is complete in this life without each other.*

PEIGAN NATION — Tuesday, Sept. 9, will be a day Joe Crow Shoe and his son Reggie will never forget. The two took off to the northwestern region of China as part of a unique cultural exchange. With them, they took three traditional teepees and other gifts from the Treaty Seven region, to present as gifts to representatives of the Kazbh peoples of China and Inner Mongolia. This trip, which represents the Treaty Seven tribes of southern Alberta, is the first phase of an exchange that will see two traditional dwellings called Yurts, brought to Alberta, by Chinese representatives next year.

Indeed, it was *together* that this remarkable couple were invited and welcomed by the world as dedicated and skilled ambassadors of peace and harmony among all persons - aborigines *and* non-aborigines alike. Joe and Josephine Crow Shoe earned the honour of being *the old man and the old woman.*

Joe Crow Shoe Sr. and his son, Reg, leave on a mission of friendship, in 1987 - a mission that prompted Rose and Reg Crow Shoe to repeat the journey in 1988.

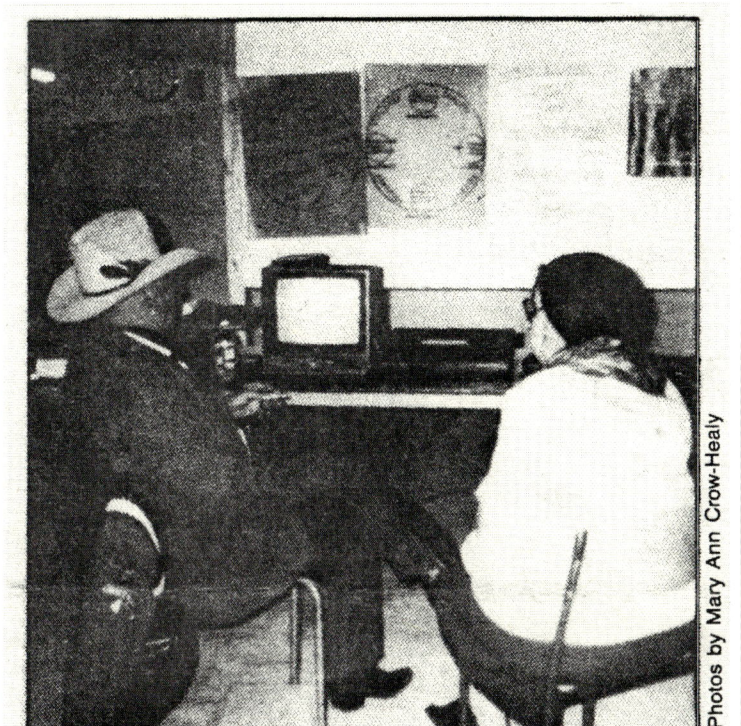

Joe and Josephine Crowshoe from the Peigan Reserve take in video presentation at the Napi Friendship Centre's first Native Awareness Week in Pincher Creek.

From the funeral service remembering the life of Joe Crow Shoe, Sr., I offer the following brief summary of a report by *Shari Narine, Sweetgrass writer, Brocket, for Alberta Aboriginal News:*

Joe died at his home surrounded by his family. His funeral was a combination of Blackfoot and English; of Christian and Indian traditions - the two communities Joe shared during his life. The Peigan Nation flag flew at half-mast as about 600 people packed the Brocket Community Hall on Nov. 2, 1999. Inside, Crowshoe's tipi hung as a backdrop and his headdress was laid in front. As the community bid farewell to their Peigan Elder, Rev. Stanley Black said Joe was a man of charity who never boasted of his accomplishments, but that those accomplishments were felt in both the native and non-native worlds. During the eulogy, Leonard Bastien, one of Crowshoe's adopted children, mentioned that Joe was a farmer by day, a leader of Blackfoot ways by night. He remarked that Joe brought knowledge from our past that is still with us today; that he always went above and beyond the call of duty, and well-beyond the boundaries of the Peigan Nation.

From the funeral service celebrating the life of Josephine Crow Shoe, I offer the following brief summary of a report by *Joyce Sasse, of the Sweetgrass staff in Pincher Creek, for Alberta Aboriginal News.*

The service was held at the Brocket Community Hall on February 5, 2002. During the proceedings, it was noted that Josephine, a wise, gentle, faithful soul, was a spiritual leader - not only sharing Joe's role in St. Cyprian's Anglican Church, but also in her own right as she committed herself to the betterment of her tribal community. It is interesting to note that Josephine had attended a residential school on the reserve, and that her marriage to Joe was the last of the arranged marriages among members of the Peigan Nation.

INDIAN DAYS
by Laura

In August, 1987, this news item from Brocket, Alberta, appeared in an Ottawa Valley newspaper.

That item served to remind the Stanger family that we were there on the Peigan Reserve for that very first *Indian Days*. We were there in southern Alberta to begin a three-year work assignment at *St. Cyprian's Indian Residential School*.

Indian Days was big news! Never before had there been such a festival on the prairies. People were thinking of little

> BROCKET — The 30th annual Indian Days was held July 31 to August 3. But the celebration marks a milestone in the sense that it was the Peigan Nation reserve who pioneered the first Indian Days way back in 1957. Although organizers said the three-day festival was a success, contenders and participants had to contend with 40-miles-an-hour gusts of winds, which caused considerable havoc in some of the events.

else. A tepee city would suddenly appear in a nearby meadow, we were told, as members of the Blackfoot Confederacy and visitors arrived from near and far for the special occasion.

Unpacking and settling into our residence, and preparing for the beginning of the 1956-57 school term demanded our attention, but we simply had to take one afternoon off to witness the local Peigan (Piikani) Nation making history. And as it turned out it was an unforgettable *first* for our family.

However, the date of that first *Indian Days festival* was not 1957 as printed in the article; it was August, 1956.

RCMP CONSTABLES
OF THE PEIGAN INDIAN RESERVE

Jerry Potts, an important part of the history of Blackfoot Country (Chapter One) died in 1896, at age 56, in Fort Macleod, Alberta. He, *Kyyokosi*, was given full honors for his 22 years of service as a special constable of the Mounties. He is also remembered as a half-breed who was welcomed into the Blackfoot Nation.

In this 1991 newspaper photograph are: Tyrone Potts, Janet Potts, and Henry Potts standing in front of a picture of their ancestor. All three are of Brocket, Alberta, and members of Peigan Band # 147; all three are proud of their heritage, and proud to serve as regular constables in Canada's national police force, the Royal Canadian Mounted Police.

News from Calgary, Alberta, as was printed in The Ottawa Citizen on May 4, 1991 reads as follows:

Three proud descendants of Mountie scout Jerry Potts, have become full-fledged members of the force that their ancestor helped lead into southern Alberta.

"I'm about ten feet tall right now," said Henry Potts, a great great-grandson of Jerry Potts, when his daughter Janet Potts and nephew Tyrone Potts became regular Royal Canadian Mounted Police constables. They had previously been special constables with power to arrest, but were not eligible for transfers nor promotions within the force.

The three members of the Peigan Indian band in southern Alberta graduated from a three-week course at the RCMP's training academy in Regina. The course was implemented by Commissioner Norman Inkster to eliminate the rank of special constable held by about 2,500 members of the force.

After graduation, the three Potts walked to a nearby RCMP museum to visit a display honoring Jerry Potts.

"I'm proud of the fact he played a part in bringing the force west," said Henry, 52, who has been with the RCMP for 14 years. Henry's first posting as a regular constable will be at Fort Macleod where Jerry Potts (his great-grandfather) died in 1896.

" Jerry Potts was a savior of sorts for the RCMP's predecessor, the North West Mounted Police," said museum curator Bill Mackay. "He led about 200 Mounties across the prairies to southern Alberta, from an area near what now is the boundary between Manitoba and Saskatchewan, and he helped choose the site for Fort Macleod."

MY ALBERTA HOME
by Judith Stanger Hendershot
former pupil at St. Cyprian's

After leaving Carcross way up north in the Yukon and bouncing along the Alaska Highway, we finally arrived at our new home. It was August 1956, and our family was now way down south in Alberta. Gone were the familiar pine trees and hulking mountains so close you could practically touch them. Instead we were greeted by endless blue sky, rolling grassland, and an imposing stairway that led up to the front door of St. Cyprian's Indian Residential School.

As luck would have it, we arrived just in time for the Indian Days Festival. A tepee village sprang up in the near distance from the school, and the sounds of rhythmic drumming provided the sound track to those first few days. At night the drum beats rocked us to sleep. Little did I know that I would soon meet girls my own age, friends like Patsy and Mildred, who could actually dance to those drums.

Indian Days Festival near St. Cyprian's

Patsy and Mildred

Soon our belongings, that Mom had carefully packed in dozens of boxes, caught up with us. What fun it was to set up housekeeping in our six room apartment that occupied about half of the main floor of the school. My brother John and I soon got used to peeking out from our bedrooms to make sure the coast was clear, before dashing across the central hall in our pyjamas. We sure didn't want anyone to see us!

My next memories are of exploring the wide open spaces that surrounded the school. John and I soon appointed ourselves caretakers of a kingdom of cats that chiefly occupied a big red barn. There were other buildings too, a granary, a hen house, a pig enclave, and the skeletal remains of a rusted Model T. Just like the other kids, we lived in the school, attended classes there, and enjoyed swinging and sliding on the playground equipment after school. However, our main job was taming those cats and thinking up cool names for their babies.

King and Queen of the cat kingdom

Snuggling with Snowball

Birds were everywhere. Red-winged blackbirds sat on fenceposts, roadrunners scurried along the dirt road, and meadowlarks chirped their cheerful songs. One of our favourite things was to walk up to "the rock" and have a picnic. This rock loomed large against the blue sky. We'd hike up there, explore a little, eat our sandwiches, and trudge back home. I heard rumours that there were snakes under that rock. Thank goodness I never saw any!

A big event in our lives was when Dad bought our family four brand-spanking-new Viscount bicycles in Pincher Creek. As I recall the girls got blue and the boys got red. Mine even had a saddle bag behind the seat. John's too. Now we could ride to the rock with our lunch riding behind us. We pedalled all over, free and easy, not having to worry about vehicles or traffic lights. Once in a while, we'd see white puffs of smoke rising above a steam locomotive chugging away in the distance.

My spiffy new wheels

John and I loved to tramp through the fields in summer and winter. I remember that we were impressed with a root cellar that had been dug into a hill. It had turnips, carrots, and other root vegetables stored inside. One day we inadvertently stumbled over a couple of nests that were hidden in the long grass. A few ducks flew up and startled us, and we felt so bad to have disturbed them.

Other creatures we'd enjoy watching were prairie dogs. They'd stand erect, surveying the landscape while also keeping an eye on us, then suddenly disappear into their burrows. Their name comes from the warning call they make that sounds very much like a dog's bark. On a slightly hilly area near the root cellar, there was a colony of these cute little guys. Maybe they were secretly stealing turnips and carrots!

In winter we'd drag our flying saucer and toboggan around looking for small hills or drifts of snow to slide down. Hills aren't very plentiful on the prairie, but we sure had fun looking. I remember that if we got cold and it was a sunny day, we'd aim the silver-coloured flying saucer at the sun and warm our faces in the reflected heat. Thank goodness the sun shines a lot in Alberta, even in winter.

John and me enjoying a massive snowdrift

Catching some winter sunshine

The wind blew almost constantly, and we soon discovered why the extremely tall chimney behind the school had heavy cables that ran from the very top to the ground to steady it as it swayed. On extremely blustery days the windows and doors would whistle and hum like an orchestra warming up. In cold weather the hot-water radiators would rattle and pop, providing the percussion.

St. Cyprian's sat on a slight rise, looking very much like a shoe box, joined to the nearby village of Brocket by a couple miles of gravel road. If Dad was driving home in the evening, I could watch the headlights all the way from over town as the station wagon moved along the road, turning left over the little bridge, then right, bouncing along the uneven surface. It was fun to watch the lights getting bigger and bigger until finally they would enter the circular driveway and stop. Then Dad would jump out and bound up the stairs to his office.

Unlike most school principals of today, Dad didn't teach in the classroom. There were teachers who did that. He was a clergyman who oversaw the daily operations of the school, as well as conducting morning and evening prayers in the little chapel on the second floor. On Sundays, he'd zip over town for services at the Anglican church and, when needed, officiate at weddings, baptisms, and funerals. Dad certainly was a busy guy.

Mom was a busy gal too. At first she was "Jill of all trades", but later she was appointed matron after Miss Higgins became ill and had to leave. She sure kept things running smoothly, teaching, and supporting the staff who cared for the approximately sixty children who lived at St. Cyprian's during the week. On Fridays the kids would head to their homes and families, then return Sunday night to be ready for the week ahead.

I was busy too because, at the age of eleven, I became an entrepreneur. Mom showed me an ad in a magazine soliciting representatives to sell Regal products. By signing up, I would receive a slim black ballpoint pen sitting in a gorgeous pink plastic rose mounted on an elegant plastic base. It was exactly what I needed for my desk. Soon the sales kit arrived, including my beautiful pen set, and I was in business! The staff became my customers, and soon orders for wrapping paper, greeting cards and handy household items came rolling in.

In a big, bright room on the second floor of the school, rows of Singer treadle sewing machines stood waiting for me and my classmates. Miss Bayne and Mom taught the class most of the time, and sometimes Miss Higgins. It was here that we learned to put in zippers, make buttonholes, install set-in sleeves, adapt patterns, and even add a lining to a jacket. These skills have come in handy over the years, but lately all I've been doing is putting patches on little boys' pants!

One day Miss Bray invited me to try my hand at beadwork. When I saw the intricate bracelets, necklaces and belts the other girls were making, I was inspired. She set up a loom for me and I used a very thin threaded needle to select beads and work them into a red and blue design. It took a while, but eventually I had a very pretty necklace.

From time to time, bulky bales of bedding and clothing would arrive from all over Canada. Service groups and churches would collect items for residential schools as a form of outreach and human kindness. Sometimes the surprise packages came with tiny sweaters, bonnets, and booties, which we'd assemble into layettes for newborn babies on the reserve. I also remember making diapers from soft white flannelette. Those were the days before disposables were invented.

Although the nursing station over town was handy for minor medical problems, the need for a dentist or eye doctor required a trip to Lethbridge. It was in that big city that I rode an escalator for the first time in a store larger than any of us had ever seen. It was neat to try things on because, up until then, we mainly bought our clothes from the Eaton's catalogue.

There was a boys playroom on one side of the school, and a girls playroom on the other, but occasionally the twain would meet. One such time was a night of square-dancing on the boys side. The whole school was there, boys, girls, staff, mom, dad, my brother, and me. For a while I really enjoyed going allemande left, allemande right, circling, and swinging with carefree abandon. Then I made a mistake. I remember turning all shades of red and running out of the room.

During our second year at St. Cyprian's, the voice of Elvis Presley reached my pre-teen ears. Roaming around the school after the kids and most of the staff had left for the summer, I discovered a radio that played all the latest tunes, including those exciting Elvis hits such as "Hound Dog" and "All Shook Up." Some folks had been to Fort Macleod or Lethbridge, to see the film "Love Me Tender." But when I heard that Elvis dies at the end of that movie, my wish to see it died too.

During our stay at St. Cyprian's, we had some special visitors. Mom's parents, Tom and Lola Harris, drove all the way from Ontario to see us. Mom turned my bedroom into a charming bed-sitting room for them, and John and I shared a room with bunk beds. I remember playing "White Christmas" on the piano at the Christmas concert while getting very hot under the incredibly bright lights attached to Grandpa's new movie camera.

One night during their visit, John and I awoke to the sounds of laughter. There in our living room were Mom, Dad, Grandpa, Grandma, and Aunt Nina, who had also arrived from Ontario, dancing with Josephine Crowshoe. Her husband Joe kept time on a round hand-held drum. Later that evening, Joe presented the drum to Grandpa, who took it back to Beachburg and hung it proudly in his den. That drum is now on display in the museum in Pembroke.

Nina Wilson and Tom and Lola Harris leaving in a snowstorm

Another time, we were excited to have visitors all the way from Edmonton. Dad's brother and family came to see us one warm summer's day. While Uncle Fred and Aunt Olive visited with Mom and Dad, John and I had fun introducing our cousins, Jim and Doug, to our cat family.

Of course we also explored the big red barn and pretended to drive the rusted Model T.

The big red barn

Princess at the pighouse

I remember the school's handyman, Andrew Brown, as a genius when it came to gardening. He tended a huge oval-shaped garden that surrounded the flagstaff at the front of the school. The weather in southern Alberta is dry and hot, but Andy used his green thumb to advantage. I can still smell the beautiful fragrance of the pretty pastel sweet peas that flourished in his garden.

John, Honey and me

We became a family of five at St. Cyprian's. John and I sucessfully convinced Mom and Dad that we needed a dog. After much research we all agreed a Beagle would be best. However, on a trip to Vancouver we visited a pet store and promptly fell in love with a tiny Cocker Spaniel puppy. He needed to stay with his mother for a while, so we returned home without him. After a long wait, Honey finally arrived by train in a special crate marked "Live Animal Handle With Love." We had absolutely no problem fulfilling those instructions!

Miss How's classroom was where the whole school congregated to watch the one and only television. She had a yellow canary and a little pet turtle that I would sometimes get to look after, feeding them and cleaning their cage and bowl. Miss How also introduced us to Kentucky Fried Chicken. It was served at a sit-down restaurant in Lethbridge, complete with china plates, real cutlery, and goblets of water. It definitely was finger lickin' good!

Mrs. McGuffie was an interesting lady with a distinctive accent who came to us from South Africa. She was a teacher, and a stickler for exercise. I recall her putting me and my classmates through our paces every day, doing her best to get us into shape. All that bending and stretching was boot camp, Alberta style.

All dressed up with Mrs. McGuffie, John and Mom

I liked Mrs. Ellis. She was warm and kind and fun. No wonder she caught the eye of Ernie Doolittle, another staff member. I was so excited when Mom told me that Edith and Ernie were getting married. In a simple ceremony, with Dad officiating and Ernie looking dapper in his cowboy shirt, they tied the knot. Imagine my surprise twenty years later at my home in Ontario, when I heard a knock at the door and when I opened it, there was Mrs. Doolittle smiling at me!

Newlyweds Edith and Ernie Doolittle

We left our prairie home at the end of the school year in 1959. As we stood on the railway platform in Brocket waiting for the dayliner, we knew it was the end of an era for us. Little did we know that St. Cyprian's was nearing the end of an era as well. Two years later, on June 30, 1961, the school closed. I was a very lucky girl to have lived such a happy and unhurried life under those endless Alberta skies.

Mildred's huge 'Easy Bake' birthday cake

Caroline, me, Mildred and our 'babies'

*My tenth birthday picnic with
Patsy, John, Caroline and Mildred*

Glennis and me after school

Mildred is the fox and I'm the second chicken from the end

An Alberta Chinook could easily turn our fort into a puddle

The echoes of those times still resonate in my life. One evening, not too long ago, I got an urgent message on my iPhone. It was from my youngest granddaughter. "I've got to interview you. Now!" was her plea. Since I was grocery shopping at the time, I pushed the cart while we texted back and forth about what my life was like when I was her age. Grace turned our interview into a speech and presented it to her grade four class at school. She got an A!

MEMORIES OF ST. CYPRIAN'S INDIAN RESIDENTIAL SCHOOL, BROCKET, ALBERTA

John Stanger, former pupil.

While I share most of the memories which my sister, Judith Hendershot, has described, I also remember:

The School:

Judy and me

A long, wide staircase led to the front door. Inside, on the first floor, was the principal's office, a suite of rooms (on both sides of the main hallway) where the principal and his family lived, the school office, a primary classroom and a staff room. On the second floor was the chapel, a sewing room and the senior classroom. The boys and girls dormitories and staff rooms were on the third floor. In the basement was the kitchen (with a walk-in freezer and refrigerator and huge institutional propane cook stoves), the laundry room (with institutional sized washers and dryers), the boiler room (for the furnace and boiler to heat water which was circulated to radiators to heat the school), and boys and girls play rooms.

The School Farm

For many years the older boys at St. Cyprian's spent half their school day working on the school farm and receiving training in agriculture, gardening, and raising cattle. These activities resulted in the production of essentially all of the flour, meat, vegetables, butter and eggs needed to feed students and staff. While the boys were engaged in farming activities, the older girls acquired skills in cooking, baking, laundry and sewing.

When we arrived at St. Cyprian's the school farm was being phased out, and in 1957 the land was returned to the Piikani for their use, but I remember:

- the big red barn where two huge black draft horses lived and where we would climb on the mounds of loose hay. In the cold weather a hole had to be chopped in the ice of a water trough so that the horses could drink;
- gathering eggs in the chicken coop;

- a pigsty and a couple of very large white pigs;
- some of the boys riding on top of a pickup truck full of turnips which I think they had just harvested;
- a root house with a door dug into the side of a hill which had been used to store potatoes; turnips and other root vegetables;
- looking through the window of my first floor classroom and seeing beef cattle being herded;

- trying to put about 16 farm cats in the cab of the farm pickup truck and then letting them go again;

- playing house with my sister Judy;
- watching a chestnut riding-type horse for hours and wishing I had the courage to jump on his back. I never did.

Television

I remember seeing television for the first time at St. Cyprian's. Each of the school staff members had a room to live in within the school. I remember watching a heavyweight boxing title fight between Ingemar Johansson and Floyd Patterson with my Dad and Mr. Doolittle in Mr. Doolittle's room on his tiny television. In spite of constant attempts to improve it, the picture was so bad that you could hardly see what was happening. In any case, we could hear the announcer and history tells us that:

> *After a series of title defences against fringe contenders (Hurricane Jackson, Pete Rademacher, Roy Harris and Brian London), Patterson met Ingemar Johansson of Sweden, the number one contender, in the first of three fights. Johansson triumphed over Patterson on June 26, 1959, with the referee Ruby Goldstein stopping the fight in the third round after the Swede had knocked Patterson down seven times. Johansson became Sweden's first World Heavyweight Champion, thus becoming a national hero as the first European to defeat an American for the title since 1933.*

Darryll, Kenneth, Gerald, Cliford:

The boys playground was on one side of the school while the girls was on the other side. I liked to play on the teeter-totters and slide with Darryll, Kenneth, Gerald and Clifford.

The playground was also equipped with a "bucking bronco" ride which was a steel 45 gallon drum suspended by chains between four posts. We would each take turns trying to stay sitting on the barrel while the other guys made it buck by pulling on the chains.

While we pretended to be wrestling for the camera, Kenneth Yellow Horn and I were actually playing catch with the football.

Sometimes I would tag along with Judy and her friends. On this occasion we were going for a picnic.

Joe Crow Shoe Junior:

Joe Crow Shoe Junior was a student at the school. He was older than I was but he liked to tell me about his horses, and I liked to listen. In those days I had an infatuation with Quarter Horses. Here are pictures of Joe and his horses.

Just after we left St. Cyprian's and Southern Alberta Joe sent me this picture, taken in August, 1959, of himself (jumping onto the steer) and his horse "Whimpy" competing with Bill Collins (the other rider) of Stavely Alberta in a steer wrestling event.

On the back of the picture Joe wrote: "The horse I'm riding was the one you used to ride at the school last summer. Her name is Whimpy."

AFTER CLASS ACTIVITIES
by Laura

At *St. Cyprian's Indian Residential School* it was the regular staff members who planned and led the many activities after class, and after a day's work. The official children's groups of the *W.A.* (The Women's Auxiliary of The Anglican Church) were part of those activities -

- The *G.A.* (Girls' Auxiliary) for older girls
- The *J.A.* (Junior Girls' Auxiliary) for younger girls
- The *C.B.L.* (Church Boys' League) for older boys
- The *J.B.L.* (Junior Boys' League) for younger boys
- The *Little Helpers* for boys and girls not yet old enough for one of the other groups.

Each of those groups had specific goals and activities which are well-reported in *Cyprian's Way*. Each group member proudly wore the official uniform to meetings and area festivals, and worked to earn various badges towards completion of his or her specific responsibilities.

We have only a few pictures of some of the groups to include here.

John Stanger in his C.B.L uniform and Judith Stanger in her J.A. uniform.

Edith Ellis (later, Edith Doolittle) leader of the J.A.

J.A. girls

G.A. group

Laura Stanger, leader of the C.B.L.

C.B.L. boys of the St. Andrew Band

C.B.L. boys of the St. Peter Band

C.B.L. boys of the St. James Band

C.B.L boys on parade

The school also encouraged other group participation, whenever and wherever leadership was available: Army Cadets, Girl Guides, 4-H Club, sewing, handicrafts, manual training, physical training, dance, sports, music, and a choir of boys and girls.

A group of choir girls and their leader, Lorraine Higgins and their pastor Rev. Stanger, after a service at St. Cyprian's Church in the village of Brocket.

AFTERWORD
by
John Stanger

OUR CANADIAN FAMILY

By John Stanger, former pupil at St. Cyprian's

In the Beginning:

Cultural differences between aboriginal and non-aboriginal Canadians developed over thousands of years during a time when the people of North America were isolated from those of Asia and Africa.

Man did not appear in North America until Homo sapiens had developed and was wide spread through the Eastern Hemisphere. These people, who were the ancestors of today's Canadian Indigenous peoples, migrated from Eastern Siberia across the Bering Land Bridge to present day Alaska around 40,000 - 17,000 years ago when lower sea levels resulted in a broad highway between Asia and North America. This was the first stage of human habitation in the Americas. For thousands of years, the sea level was from 50 to 300 feet lower than it is now because much of the water that might have been in the oceans was locked up in glaciers which had buried much of Alberta under a kilometre of ice. As the great ice masses finally melted, billions of gallons of trapped water were released and the sea level rose and covered the land bridge. The Bering Strait split the Asian and North American continents into two solitudes. As a result, the people of North America were isolated from the peoples of the "Old World" until the coming of the Europeans in the 15th century.

Because of the absence of edible food plants in many locations and at different seasons of the year, early man in North America was in most cases an eater of animal flesh and consequently a hunter. Because he was a hunter he was also a wanderer, following the herds of wooly mammoth, giant sloth, bison and big horn elk. His weapons and tools were of stone, bone and wood. These people who had to struggle to survive in North America, evolved at a later date than their Old World counterparts in Africa and Asia who were well blessed with resources, fertile soil and a moderate climate

The development of cities in Africa and Asia was synonymous with the rise of civilization in about 3500 BC. These societies developed a central government, a complex economy and social structure, sophisticated language and writing systems, and distinct culture and religions. Around 1000, the population of Europe increased greatly as new technological and agricultural innovations allowed trade to flourish and crop yields to increase. An important geographic factor in the rise of Europe was the Mediterranean Sea which, for millennia, functioned as a maritime superhighway fostering the exchange of goods, people, ideas and inventions. As complex civilizations arose in the Eastern Hemisphere, indigenous societies in North America remained relatively simple.

Extensive European colonization of the Americas began in 1492 when Spain sponsored a major exploration led by Christopher Columbus. The French founded Quebec on the St. Lawrence in 1604, the English settled on the James River in 1607.

When Europeans came to North America in the 15th century, their modern culture clashed with the more primitive way of life of the natives who were still gathering, hunting and fishing.

As the traditional way of life of Canada's aborigines was ending with colonization and the decimation of the great buffalo herds, the early missionaries, the churches, and ultimately the Government of Canada began to try to provide Canada's native people with an education which would enable them to contribute to, and prosper in, a modern Canadian economy.

Indian Residential Schools:

> *Use of the term "Indian" originated with Christopher Columbus who thought that he had arrived in the East Indies while seeking Asia. The use of the name "Indian" has served to imply some kind of racial or cultural unity for the aboriginal peoples of the Americas. Once created, the unified "Indian" was codified in law, religion, and*

> *politics. The unitary idea of "Indians" was not originally shared by indigenous peoples, but many over the last two centuries have embraced the identity. The term "Indian" does not include certain other indigenous peoples such as the Inuit peoples. The terms "Indian" and "Eskimo" have largely fallen into disuse in Canada and are commonly considered pejorative.*

Hospice St Joseph, the first Indian residential school in Alberta, opened at Lac La Biche in 1862. In 1911, after successive Parliaments had endorsed the policy of requiring native children to attend residential schools, new contracts were negotiated between the government and the church organizations which ran the schools. Between 1911 and 1951 the number of Indian residential schools increased to more than 80. By 1930, 75% of First Nations children between the ages of 7 and 15 years were enrolled in residential schools. By 1945 there were 9149 students in the residential school system across Canada. These numbers continued to increase rapidly in the early 1950's. By 1952, Ottawa was responsible for hiring all teachers and had complete control over in-class curriculum, which was the prevailing standard in the public schools.

After World War II, however, Ottawa began to question the prevailing practice of church-state run education for aboriginal peoples. The policies of the government of Canada towards Aboriginal education finally changed when the costs of the residential schools escalated beyond its desire to sustain them, and when it was lobbied by Aboriginal groups to stop the segregated education of their children. As a result, by the early 1960s, the government's new policy was that every effort should be made to keep Indian children in schools that afforded them the ability to return to their families at the end of each school day, and that the residential school system should be shut down.

Consistent with its new policy, and despite objections from the Piikani community, the government closed **St. Cyprian's** Indian residential school on June 30, 1961. Enrolment had fallen to 35 pupils in the school's final year as more children became day students. As the replacement for St. Cyprian's, and the former day school, the Peigan Indian Day School, which was operated by the Anglican Missionary Society of the Church of England in Canada (MSCC), opened in the fall of 1961 with first year enrolment of 90 students in the elementary grades. This school continued until 1964 when Piikani children were transferred to a new elementary public school in Brocket. In the mid-1980s, the local Piikani band assumed control of the former day school and, in 1997, these facilities were expanded into the all-grade Piikani Nation Secondary School. The Piikani Nation Secondary School is now operated by the local Indian band.

Since this new policy to educate all Indian children in day schools could not be implemented overnight, the residential schools did what they could to accommodate the new policy by providing services based on the specific needs of their students. Some schools remained full residential schools to those students who were too far from home to travel each day. Others became day schools from which the students returned to their families at night. Still others were only a boarding house for children who attended primary and secondary day schools in the local communities.

During this time, the purpose of the residential schools also changed from the education of all Aboriginal students, to being responsible for the education and welfare of "orphans and children from disrupted homes." The schools became repositories for children who were considered to be at risk for neglect and abuse within their homes. Many of these students were eventually placed in foster care through new child and family service agencies run by both the federal government and the Aboriginal groups themselves.

Aboriginal education was secularized in 1969 when the federal government ended its partnership with the churches.

In the early 1900s it was believed that residential schools were the best way, or perhaps the only way, to provide an education to an aboriginal population which was sparsely spread over thousands of square miles. Over time societies often make decisions that, as conditions change and moral standards shift, are later deemed unacceptable. Canadians today consider that the segregated education of aborigines in residential schools was inappropriate. As a result, apologies and restitution payments have been offered on behalf of those who are no longer around. In his 1993 address to the National Native Convocation, the Anglican Primate, Archbishop Michael Peers offered an apology for the Church's role in being a part of the Indian residential school system. On January 7, 1998 then Indian Affairs Minister Jane Stewart apologized saying "For those of you who suffered this tragedy, we are deeply sorry," and announced a $350-million fund for "healing initiatives that will be run by aboriginal communities. The money will be spent on programs such as counseling and language training." In December, 2007 a class-action court settlement was reached with a total value of about $5 billion. It included provisions for payments to some 80,000 native Indians; provisions for a $125 million aboriginal healing fund, $100 million for legal fees, $60 million for a five-year Truth and Reconciliation process to document the legacy of the schools and $20 million for commemorative projects. On June 11, 2008 Prime Minister Stephen Harper rose in the House of Commons to deliver a formal apology.

Over the years, my family and I have become increasingly incredulous that our experiences at the St. Cyprian's and Chooutla Indian residential schools (described in this book and in *Laughing Water* by Laura Harris Stanger) are apparently not typical of those of all, or even a majority of, others.

> *My mother (Laura May Stanger, nee Harris) and father (Charles Thomas Stanger) met while serving in the Royal Canadian Air Force and were married in Edmonton on January 12, 1946. Following Dad's graduation from the St. John's College of Arts, Science and Theology, University of Manitoba, Winnipeg in the spring of 1950, Mom, Dad, sister Judy and I moved to Whitehorse where Dad worked as Interim Rector, Christ Church, Whitehorse from July 23, 1950 until June 17, 1951. Dad was*

principal of the Chooutla Indian Residential School near Carcross, Yukon from June, 1951 until we moved to St. Cyprian's IRS in August, 1956. My family and I lived at St. Cyprian's Indian Residential School near Brocket in southern Alberta from August, 1956 until August, 1959. My earliest memories are of the eight years our family spent living and working in these Indian residential schools.

In my experience, education in the Indian residential schools was provided with compassion and caring. I remember enjoying many social activities while celebrating our cultural differences and building friendships. Some of these activities and friendships are reflected in the pictures which have been reproduced in this book. The objective was not to replace native language and culture (indeed the students of St. Cyprian's lived only a few miles from the school and went home on weekends) but to provide aboriginal Canadians with the same education and opportunities as non-aborigines. In addition to reading, writing and arithmetic, students were given a good understanding of Christian beliefs and were involved in music, drama, dance and sports. Competitive residential school hockey, football and baseball teams gave students opportunities to see other schools and communities. During all of these activities students gained self-confidence and learned to talk to and get along with other people.

Rather than feeling embarrassed or regretful for having been associated with a system which caused unintended harm to some of the children it was trying to help, the former teachers and staffs of Canada's Indian residential schools should feel satisfaction for a job well done in service to their church and country, and proud of the many children who flourished under their guidance. Many students developed a love of learning and pursued their education beyond the residential school system. By 1959 The number of children in grades 9 to 13 increased from none in 1945 to 2144 in 1959. In the next decade it rose to 6834.

This too is an important part of the history of Canada's Indian residential schools.

Today:

Aborigines and non-aborigines have been living together, in what is now Canada, for over 400 years. Although we come from different backgrounds, we are together now a family of Canadians. The struggle to define the relationship of aboriginal and non-aboriginal Canadians to each other and to the rest of the world, which began in the 1600's with the colonization of the New World, continues to this day. It is our hope that today's decisions will result in a better tomorrow for all Canadians.

THE TWENTY-THIRD PSALM

(as interpreted from native sign language that once was nearly universal between various aboriginal tribes)

The Great Father above is Shepherd Chief. I am His, and with Him, I want not.

He throws out to me a rope, and the name of the rope is Love.

He draws me to where the grass is green and the water is good; I eat and lie down satisfied.

Sometimes my heart is weak and I fall down, but He lifts me up again and draws me into a good road. His name is Wonderful.

Sometime, it may be soon, it may be longer, it may be a long, long time; He will draw me into a place between mountains. It is dark there but I'll draw not back for it is there between those mountains that the Shepherd Chief will meet me, and the hunger I have felt in my heart all through this life will be satisfied.

Sometimes He makes the love rope into a whip, but afterwards He gives me a staff to lean on. He spreads a table before me with all kinds of food. He puts His hands upon my head, and all the tired is gone. My cup He fills 'till it runs over.

What I tell you is true. I lie not. Those roads that are away ahead will stay with me through this life, and afterwards I will go to live in the Big Tepee and sit down with the Shepherd Chief forever.

Other books by Laura

Their Land of Promise

Although they grew up a mere fifteen miles apart, two young homestead adults meet by chance in the fledgling Lower Canada of the mid-eighteen hundreds. Their parents, however, had arrived into that wilderness area a quarter-century earlier from distant and culturally-diverse parts of the world. 'Their Land Of Promise' travels to those distant lands; breathes life and love into those parents again; shares their problems; learns their dreams; and eventually it travels with them into Britain's colony, a land full of dense wilderness forests - forests the newcomers challenge with a Bible in one hand and an axe in the other.

Pastures Green

On the pages of her book Laura May Harris weaves a memorial to five generations of men and women who carved out a life on the family homestead. This very personal family perspective chronicles the lives of some of the earliest pioneers and their descendants - many of whom have contributed their memories to this rich anthology. She aptly chose this Muriel Strode quotation to describe the philosophy of her forebearers: "We will not follow where the path may lead, but we will go where there is no path, and we will leave a trail."

Echo

Born in 1924, Laura May Harris uses her vivid memory and unique writing skills to create a series of rustic tales which not only illustrate family life at the beginning of the 20th century, during the Roaring Twenties and the Great Depression, but also illuminates the author's own personal journey from farm to forces to frontier. And anchoring those vignettes are various adventures unfolding during the same era, but well-beyond her own doorstep. Echo is a thoroughly enjoyable read. For today's youth, it allows them to walk a mile in the footsteps of their grandparents; for today's seniors resting up for the next lap of life's journey, it gives them license to smile.

A Magical Visit to Hodgepodge – *New Colour Edition*

Guided by Master Magician Cameron, Laura Harris Stanger creates a lovely collection of stories for her great-grandchildren. Besides being entertaining she has given them a taste of what life was like on a Quebec farm almost eighty years ago. This collection of stories are charmingly illustrated by her great-grandchildren. A family heirloom but an entertaining 'read' for all young children.

Laughing Water

Laughing Water whisks a reader back in time to when the First Nations people of northwestern Canada led a nomadic life as fur traders; back to the earliest missionaries who introduced formal education to our first Canadians; and back to when Canadian governments and churches shared this responsibility. Laughing Water is proud to invite its readers to read words written by some of the students and staff of the Chooutla Indian Residential School in their 1955-56 school paper, The Chooutla Grayling. Laura Harris Stanger devoted many years of her adult life to working in Indian residential schools, and she fondly remembers her years at Chooutla as a special time when her skills were challenged and stretched and her life's values enriched by the people of the Yukon.